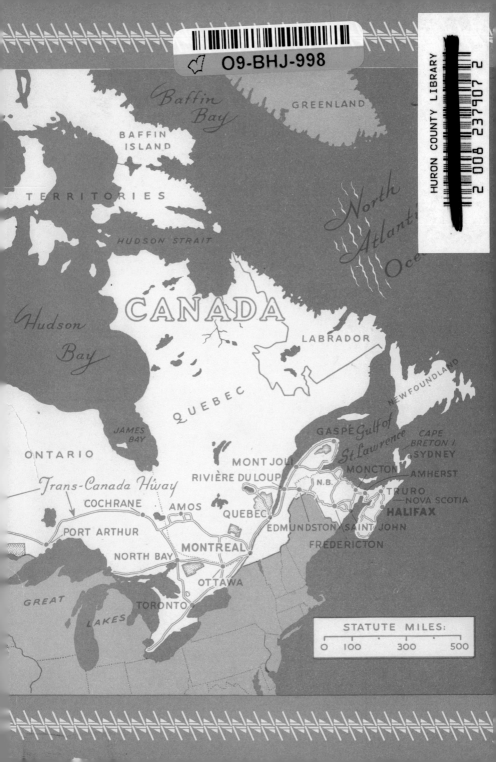

Baffin
Bay

GREENLAND

BAFFIN
ISLAND

T E R R I T O R I E S

North
Atlantic
Ocean

HUDSON STRAIT

CANADA

LABRADOR

Hudson

Bay

NEWFOUNDLAND

QUEBEC

JAMES
BAY

GASPÉ Gulf of
St. Lawrence CAPE
BRETON I.
SYDNEY

ONTARIO

MONT JOLI

RIVIÈRE DU LOUP

MONCTON AMHERST

N.B.

TRURO
NOVA SCOTIA

Trans-Canada Hway

COCHRANE

AMOS

QUEBEC

HALIFAX

PORT ARTHUR

EDMUNDSTON SAINT JOHN

FREDERICTON

MONTREAL

NORTH BAY

OTTAWA

GREAT

TORONTO

LAKES

STATUTE MILES:

0   100   300   500

You Must See Canada

BOOKS BY CECIL CARNES

YOU MUST SEE CANADA

YOU MUST GO TO MEXICO (with Fred Carnes)

SECRET MISSION SUBMARINE (with Lieutenant N. L. A. Jewell)

AMERICAN GUERRILLA (with Captain Douglas M. Smith)

LAST MAN OFF WAKE ISLAND (with Colonel Walter L. J. Baylor)

DOWN THE RIVER OF DEATH (with L. V. Cummings)

JIMMY HARE, NEWS PHOTOGRAPHER

JOHN L. LEWIS: LEADER OF LABOR

YOU MUST SEE
CANADA

by

CECIL CARNES

ZIFF-DAVIS PUBLISHING COMPANY

CHICAGO · NEW YORK

ZIFF DAVIS
PUBLISHING COMPANY
Chicago · New York · Los Angeles
★
ZIFF-DAVIS LIMITED
London

PRINTED IN THE UNITED STATES OF AMERICA
AMERICAN BOOK–STRATFORD PRESS, INC., NEW YORK

FOR

*Mrs. Jack Cotts, my sister, whose
selflessness does not call attention*

Foreword

LAST YEAR the critics were good enough to characterize *You Must Go to Mexico* as a new kind of travel book for Americans: informative, brief, lighthearted, and concerned with present-day things. Because of this reception for the Mexico book I have spent many months and traveled many thousands of miles gathering information for *You Must See Canada*. It is impossible to cover this new subject with the thoroughness with which we gave you Mexico. In the case of that small country I was able to mention almost every hotel tourists could reach in their own automobiles. There are many thousands of such places in Canada. Canada is so big that if it were possible to take Mexico and drop it into the center of Canada's "unexplored" area, experienced hikers couldn't find our Latin neighbor in a week's walking. Canada's geographical area is second only to Russia's in the world. It is larger than the whole of Europe. Ontario, not the largest province, is twice the size of the state of Texas, despite tall talk from Deep in the Heart of the Claghorns.

Those of you who laughed your way through Mexico with my brother and me may wonder whether the Canadians have a sense of humor as you read this book. They have. But they are not gay. Life is even a bit more real and earnest for them than for us in the United States. You'll find many a passage which I hope will bring a chuckle, but please remember one doesn't kid a great people like the Canadians. They have come out of this second great war as one of the top world powers. Canada is third in sea power, fourth in air power, and first in the production of nickel, newsprint, asbestos, and platinum; it also possesses important deposits of some other materials about which little can at present be written.

Canada must be pretty near first, too, in developing pleasant, intelligent, hard-working men and women to help a foreign writer compile the materials of which a book are made. I owe appreciation to the following:

Walter Thompson, of the Canadian National Railways, the only super-portly man I know who actually exudes personality, charm, poise, and knowledge. (Mr. Thompson "arranged" things on King George's tour of Canada shortly before the war, and I'll wager the King was most impressed.)

George Herbert Lash, assistant to Mr. Thompson and one of the friendliest and most brilliant men I've ever met. When government ownership of railways results in the hiring of men like Mr. Lash and Mr. Thompson it is powerful propaganda for nationalization.

John Noel, Joe Fountain, Bruce Boreham, Claude Melançon, Frank E. D. McDowell, G. S. Towill, F. R. Sayer, A. A. Leaman, and J. H. Norton, all employees of the Canadian National Railways.

J. Edgar March, of the Canadian Pacific Railways, jolly and efficient, living proof that public relations pays an employer. And Norman Mackintosh of his staff, mighty researcher.

D. Leo Dolan, Director of the Canadian Travel Bureau and all of the provincial tourist bureau personnel, but especially Miss Mary Ainslie, R. A. McMullen, Will R. Bird, Maurice Hebert, Horace M. Block, Dan Campbell and T. J. Courtney.

CECIL CARNES

Contents

· I ·

Under Leaning Sails in Nova Scotia

HALFWAY BETWEEN the Equator and the North Pole, on Knock Him Down Street in Halifax where your watch is set to Atlantic time, I met Lord Brooklyn, taxicab driver and guide extraordinary.

Some people, His Lordship opined, are skeptics. They'd rather call him by the name on his license, plain Harry MacDonald. This, though he swore he could trace ancestry back to one of the original baronets of Nova Scotia created in 1621 by King James I of England, in furtherance of a real-estate deal. That name of Brooklyn? It didn't refer to Brooklyn, the little town across from Manhattan, but a sweet and proper coastal city southwest of Halifax once known as Herring Cove. Good thing they changed the name, His Lordship said. Lord Herring Cove just wouldn't seem right.

"Until the *Almanach de Gotha* catches up with the authenticity of my title, and maybe even afterwards," said His Lordship, sneaking in a little sip of amber fluid out of a monogrammed milk bottle, "I'll be happy telling visitors about Halifax, capital of the peninsula province.

"Imagine a hard sponge in the shape of a lobster. That's Nova Scotia, with the claws Cape Breton Island. This eastern coastline is receding and now Nova Scotia is almost an island. The sea pervades it, rises at points all through it, smashes at it from the Atlantic side, beats upon it almost everywhere. Practically surrounds it. The ocean tells almost the entire story of Nova Scotia. Fishing, boat-building, sailing everything from a skiff to the largest thing afloat; the sea is the explanation of everything here, and the beginning and the end. A pitcher of salt water would be the perfect blood transfusion for any old resident.

"Now then consider Halifax. It, too, is almost an island. Two long arms of the sea are extended around it in perpetual promise of embrace. But mark you well those arms never close, like a doting mother's. That would be cloying, confining. Rather the sea is a mistress to rough old Halifax. She never denies him, and when the other harbors are chock full of ice, Halifax puts his mistress to work even more. One of these long arms runs right through the town and on the other side extends into a basin, deep and wide enough for the entire British fleet to drop anchor. Here the sea has taken care of her own. Even among Nova Scotia's almost perfect harbors—let's include Shelburne and Sydney—Halifax stands out. Its approaches are narrow and easily defended. In two world wars booms across the entrances kept submarines out. Convoys made up inside, sallied forth, shipped the goods.

"Here between those two arms of ocean, dominating everything, is the Citadel. This street here, once called Knock Him Down Street, is its base. It got its name when it ran between the north and south barracks for the military personnel, and the houses along here were either grog shops or brothels. Where you are standing right now, scores of very famous men have stood. William, Lord Clarence, later King William IV, stood there, surrounded by his pals just before they took off for Water Street down below, and a round of all the taverns. And General Wolfe, who took Quebec. He must have looked like a redheaded Ichabod Crane as he bounced around here getting his crooked nose into everything.

"And Admiral Lord Nelson. He was here on many occasions and they say he had a flaming love affair here, too, just as he did in Quebec City and perhaps Montreal. Sea air must have whetted certain of his appetites, sailor-wise. And the Duke of Kent, later to become father of the illustrious queen, Victoria, God bless her soul, he walked here at five o'clock of the morning, to see that everyone was out of bed and heading for the parade ground. Stickler for promptitude, he was, even though he'd been out carousing around till all hours with his mistress, Julie de St. Laurent. He carried punctuality to extremes, putting watches into walls where they could never be wound and ordering a huge four-sided clock for Citadel Hill. But the maker didn't believe in watching the clock. He didn't deliver the works until after the Duke had sailed away."

Lord Brooklyn coughed, took a little more soothing sirup, and pointed out the general direction of Hollis Street. Over there, he said, Captain John Moore had lived while an officer in the garrison, he who was later "buried darkly at dead of night" on the ramparts of Corunna. Here on the cobbled streets so recently trod by intrepid airmen, paratroopers, marines and jacktars, Edward Cornwallis, cousin of the nobleman who led the British to defeat at Yorktown, took command of the "rabble" which had been enlisted to hew this city by fiat out of the wilderness so that England could protect the New England Coast from the French. And here Sir Samuel Cunard walked barefoot and with the dreams which resulted in a great steamship line.

On the way back to my hotel, Lord Brooklyn showed me Old St. Paul's Church, which not only is the oldest Protestant institution in Canada, but the principal repository of dignity in the city of Halifax.

Sitting in one of its high-backed pews in the solemn half-light it was no trick at all to bring back the days of grandeur when redcoated transmission belts for England's fame sat here and gave thanks for the winning of ancient battles. The historian who bleats with joy as he unravels family skeins can make of St. Paul's crypts and monuments a minor Canterbury or Chester. Indeed, the place was meant to be patterned after Marylebone Chapel, but in its original form was a copy of St. Peter's of Vere Street, London.

"These fine oak panels and pine sheathings, which have lasted since July or August, 1750, almost two hundred years, came from New England," said my taxicab guide. "There was a sawmill here, sure. But unless Eddie Cornwallis wanted to run it himself there wasn't any work done. They went to Boston for their lumber, just as they went to Massachusetts for troops when it came to fighting. But slowly there was a great switch in population. The riffraff who exchanged residence in England's jails to become 'colonists' because of the free food and rum decided they liked New England cities better: these cities offered them greater comfort, more chance for grifting. And the thrifty New Englanders saw a chance to get in on pioneering's ground floor again, this time subsidized by the British government, which had a job of work to get done here, setting up a naval base to protect the North Atlantic. So the British rabble moved to the colonies down the coast.

"The more sturdy stock which replaced them were, naturally, sympathetic to the rebel cause. But a comparative handful of armed Yorkshiremen between them and an American column kept Nova Scotia loyal to the crown."

I remembered reading about this in the incomparable

book *His Majesty's Yankees* by Thomas H. Raddall, the Nova Scotian author.

Across the street from my hotel, the Nova Scotian, in a pretty little park, I found the statue of Cornwallis, who looked severe, as befits a young man of thirty-seven given the job of creating a lasting bastion of empire. Standing at the base of this monument and looking at Massey Rhind's fine likeness, one might almost believe Edward Cornwallis would not be amazed at anything he saw were he able to attend the celebration of the two-hundredth anniversary of the city, June 21 to August 11, 1949. But if he were to exclaim at anything it would probably be at the view of things from this pedestal for his own likeness. The trams and cabs which run alongside the park and the magnificent hotel (run by the Canadian National Railways: single rooms from $3.50; double from $5.00) with corridors connecting to ocean piers and the railway terminal, encompass almost everything modern except the radar with which, according to rumor, the Royal Canadian Mounted Police keep tabs on possible rumrunners in these modern times. It isn't difficult to imagine Cornwallis sweeping his long black cape around him, jamming his floppy black hat over his formal hairdo, folding his lanky frame into a taxicab and saying, "To the Grand Parade grounds." And there, like any other tourist, exhibiting interest in the Citadel, monstrous, ordered conglomeration of glacis, moats, firing slits, walls, flying ramparts, bastions, and garden variety casements. Edward Cornwallis would likely have gone there as the best spot from which to view the city. When his health broke in 1752 and the Founder sailed away to England, this spot was only a goat pasture and a formal parade ground ringed by a few blockhouses.

When I went there it was with Will R. Bird, author of

Historic Nova Scotia and other works. I had made an appointment for Monday, and spent Sunday in my hotel room, studying Mr. Bird's excellent pamphlets, which I advise you to write for, before your visit, to the Bureau of Information, Government of Nova Scotia, Halifax, N. S. Maps furnished by this same agency will show you how best to get to Nova Scotia. During the summer there is a large choice of steamers, which run from both New York and Boston to Yarmouth, from where you continue by Dominion Atlantic Railway, serving the Land of Evangeline, or Canadian National Railways to anywhere on the south shore. If you brought your car you may drive out of Yarmouth on Route 3 for a beautiful trip through famous tuna and other Atlantic Ocean fishing ports, or take Route 1 through historical Annapolis Royal and other off-Bay-of-Fundy towns. There are direct New York to Halifax sailings, too, on which you may bring along your automobile as freight.

Motoring from the United States you will be able to take advantage of Halifax's fine tourist courts, and on your $100 customs exemptions on purchases, load up with everything from Irish linens, Scotch tweeds, diamonds (yes, Halifax is a good place to buy diamonds!) to Nova Scotian amethysts or a hooked-rug cummerbund. If wheeling your own car from New York, you can take Routes 1 and 2, through Boston, Portland, Moncton, and Truro. If from Montreal or Quebec, Route 2, via Rivière du Loup. And if you wish to visit the south rim of the Gaspé or skirt the Bay de Chaleur, or if for any reason you wish to drive farther north, take Route 2 to Mont Joli, then Route 6 via Campbellton, New Brunswick, and then Route 11, at Moncton. These are all good roads. After making connections with the New York, New Haven and Hartford train out of New York, there is a through train from Boston

Smallest of the nine Canadian provinces, Prince Edward Island is a land where blue sea and sky contrast vividly with red soil and green fields and life moves at a leisurely pace. *Above:* Tignish, a typical little community; *below:* a corner of the Island's rolling landscape.

Halifax Harbor from Citadel Hill. Note Old Town Clock in the tower.

St. Paul's Church, Halifax, the oldest Protestant church in Canada.

Fishermen haul in a big tuna at Wedgeport, Nova Scotia.

Freighter under construction at Lunenburg, Nova Scotia.

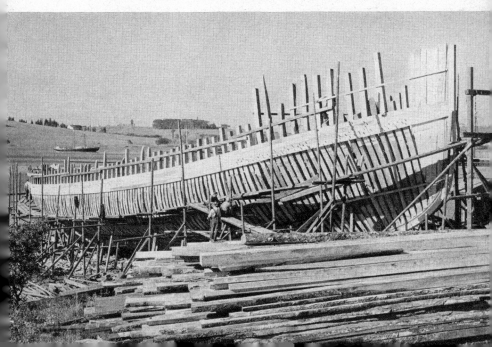

Exhibit of hooked rugs at Sydney, Nova Scotia.

Winter in Nova Scotia. Hauling logs over ice.

Fort Anne, Annapolis Royal, Nova Scotia. Cannon from the original fort in foreground.

Statue of Evangeline in Evangeline Memorial Park at Grand Pré, Nova Scotia.

Peggy's Cove, Nova Scotia. *Above:* view of waterfront; *below:* a typical lighthouse perched on the barren rock.

←

At Lunenburg, Nova Scotia. *Above:* fishing craft in harbor; *below:* oxen carry load of dried cod to fish plant.

One of the many old wooden covered bridges that serve as landmarks in Nova Scotia.

The Cabot Trail winds among the hills, hugging the shore.

over the Boston & Maine Railway from Quebec and Ontario points via Montreal. Both the Canadian National and the Canadian Pacific operate daily trains, sometimes offering excursion rates.

You may also fly into Canada from the United States. If you come in your own plane you must first notify the Canadian Customs authorities of your estimated time of arrival and receive a reply collect. This is true in all instances unless you wish to make your first landing at Dorval Airport, Montreal. No charge will be made unless your arrival is so timed that transportation and overtime must be paid for inspecting officials—in which case you pay it. The Halifax Airport, located conveniently close to the city, is up-to-date in most respects. The provincial map you can get on request will show distances to the Nova Scotian border from your home town (or the nearest large city to it) and preferred routes. (Example: From Indianapolis, Indiana, via Sandusky and Buffalo, 1,594 miles.) It will also tell you how far it is from Halifax to almost any port in the world.

In Halifax, the best hotels are the Lord Nelson, which is largest, and like the Nova Scotian, has a fine location: Spring Garden Road on Highways 1, 2, and 3, and just opposite the Public Gardens and near to the Citadel, both prime tourist attractions (rates approximately the same as the Nova Scotian); the Halifax, on Hollis Street, quiet, yet dignified, rates modest; the Carleton, on Argyle Street, across from Old St. Paul's (and this same management operates Green Acres, charming roadside teahouse with overnight cottages, at near-by Waverley); Hillside Hall, a quiet residential place, excellent for families, and with low prices. There are other, smaller hotels, and if you write the Bureau of Information they will supply the names and rates of private homes, which charge an average of $1.50 a

person a day. At each of the great hotels, meals are exceptionally good, and comparatively cheap. Food, in general,
is cheaper in Canada than in the United States. Excellent
lobster is available, and famous Chester scallops. But other
than at hotels I found eating places rather uninspired.
A visitor's permit, at twenty-five cents, will allow you to
buy weakened gin or whiskey at four government liquor
stores in the city.

This matter of where you can get liquor, and under
what conditions, I found very confusing throughout Canada. The rules vary from hypocrisy to prohibition and are
almost as silly as in the United States. But in Canada there
is this difference: the tourist trade ranks as the third
industry in several provinces. A visitor might arrive in a
Canadian city, large enough to be a grown-up town, and
discover that he can't get a drink—on his vacation! Perhaps some day this matter will be handled on an international level, reciprocally, so that any Canadian visitor to
the United States, or American going to Canada, at the
border will be handed permits allowing him to purchase
vacation spirits.

I had come to Canada again to travel between 20,000
and 25,000 miles in a few months by every means
of conveyance known to man except the pogo stick. My
idea: setting down why Canada is the world's greatest
tourist attraction; why Americans spend more than a
quarter-billion dollars a year there; where to go; what
there is to see; why you should bother to see it; and some
idea of what it might cost. And now I was ready for my
friendly tour with Will Bird and, as *Time* magazine
would put it, no dodo he.

A fine blending of the scholarly and the convivial type,
Mr. Bird told me what tourists do in Halifax. "They go to
the nine or ten movies we have in the city," he said with

a little laugh, "just as though they had come all that distance for the purpose. But maybe it relaxes them. Then they go to band concerts at the Public Gardens, or dancing at one of the rowing clubs, or they just walk along the piers. You can see the unloading of strange and romantic goods from all over the world. Then, too, it seems nearly every visitor wants to hear personal stories of the great explosion, fire, and blizzard of 1917. There are few Haligonians of middle age but who have personal recollections of that disaster, which took 2,000 lives and wounded several thousands more, mostly by blinding."

We drove to the spot overlooking Bedford Narrows where the *Imo* was when she crashed into the *Mont Blanc.* "There was a blue deck halo over the *Mont Blanc,*" said Mr. Bird, "a blue shroud of doom. And then she let go with the nearest thing to an atomic explosion the world had then known. People all over the city looked up questioningly when the great blue incandescence flared, and met glass fragments from a hundred thousand windows when the explosion followed. That is why you see so many sightless persons in Halifax today.

"Stand here. Ahead of you is where the blast occurred. Turn directly around, and you can see where the Duc d'Anville dropped anchor 201 years ago, almost to this day, with his storm-shattered Armada which was to have won back Acadia by force of arms and then gone on to burn Boston. But the men died here from some strange malady, died by the thousands. Over there under the big trees of the Rockingham district they propped themselves up and expired. D'Anville died and then his second in command committed suicide. From this one place you can take in sites of battles which were meant to be fought somewhere else; because, of course, when D'Anville came here there was no Halifax and no one here with whom to fight."

A short time later we had gone past the Duke of Kent's old watchtower and to the summit where sits the virgin Citadel, untried by those who violently would have possessed her. This cold pile was the (eight-sided) dream of the dashing Duke.

Bird told me what you, the tourist, will be told over and over: the Duke strewed fortifications around like John D. Rockefeller used to hand out dimes; his mistress, Mme. Julie de St. Laurent, had already lost out to a drawing board as soon as the Duke spied that hill. Just the place for a fort and he'd reach into Drawer A for one which would fit—once he'd knocked off seventy feet of nature's mistake from the top. Mr. Bird hazarded that the Citadel was never breached because it was impregnable for its time. And I maintained that the fort was never built which couldn't be taken, given the officers and the pressure and the promise of loot.

Anyway, there she sits, an eighteenth-century insurance policy, all paid up and outdated. During the First World War the British incarcerated Leon Trotsky there, but let him out too soon. He fled to Europe, made peace with the Germans, and set into motion certain events which have the world fearing now that we're going to bed each night tucked in with an atomic bomb made in Omsk or Minsk. We, however, were able to put aside such thoughts and went on viewing things: a heavy ship's anchor, blown across town by the 1917 blast; the beautiful Spring Gardens; the Northwest Arm, which is a silvery needle stuck in dazzling greensward, and the Martello Tower at Point Pleasant. This fat military silo was another Duke of Kent innovation. "The theory was that round shot would bounce off a round structure," explained Mr. Bird. "Then some wise guy shot a hole right through one and they lost their vogue."

Point Pleasant Park belongs to the Crown, but is rented each year for a shilling, which is just about as cheap as 200 acres can be had that close to town. Besides, it has ten miles of shaded walks, seashore drives, bridal paths, and three forts. From the matchless Memorial Tower, a wonderful and an inspiring edifice which commemorates the establishment of representative government in Nova Scotia and is proudly "autographed" in stones and plaques by various sections of the British Commonwealth, Mr. Bird and I watched couples strolling through the birch groves of Sir Sandford Fleming Park and a few intrepid splashers swimming where the North West Arm broadens out. Not far away, he told me, there is the farm which changed hands for a reason unique in Nova Scotian history. The owner, a society woman, committed an involuntary indiscretion at a swanky dinner party. During the portentous lull which followed the considerate gentleman on her right stood up, bowed, asked her pardon, and, assuming authorship of the breach, departed. When the lady left this life she also left her farm to her benefactor. Perhaps chivalry has never been so well rewarded in matter-of-fact Halifax.

But, summing it up, the city is one of those rare Canadian municipalities where history seems always with you, yet where you do not necessarily expect others to stop their work and join in the worship at history's shrine. Quebec, for instance, demands everybody's time in order to be Quebec, the big tourist attraction. Halifax can be workaday, drab in spots, and yet thrill and enlighten you, all on a summer's day. The chief petty officer who told me, coming down to Halifax on the train, "There's nothing down there; you'll be glad to get away," was a sincere but faulty reporter. Yet, who could expect a sailor, home from the sea, to seek enjoyment on a bench at Point Pleasant, overlooking the harbor and the cliff of York Redoubt and the lighthouse, the speckled woods?

One might imagine, though, that any sailor would thrill to some stories of Halifax and the sea. Take the true epic of the *Tallahassee*. As Longstreth tells it in his excellent book, *To Nova Scotia:* "The Civil War was at its height in that year (1864), and Canada, who has always had a wonderful time of it when the United States is engaged in war or prohibition or similar insanity, was making a good thing of blockade-running." Among these blockade-runners was the *Tallahassee,* chased into Halifax by two Union gunboats, and after forty-eight hours, liable to internment after Queen Victoria had reluctantly and belatedly put principles ahead of pounds and politics. The gunboats lay outside the limit recognized by international law, but they effectively bottled up the *Tallahassee.* There was another entrance to Halifax harbor which, though marked on Union maps, was not even considered passable for boats of the draft of the Confederate ship: the Eastern Passage. But, with the aid of tugs and a dark night, the *Tallahassee* slipped out, brushing the foliage on both sides of the narrow, shallow, tortuous, unused channel.

But enough of old Halifax. We have much to see in Nova Scotia, so we'll scoot out Route 3 and go around clockwise, with short side trips. The first of these is one of the most notable in all Canada, that to Peggy's Cove. You branch to the left off Route 3 a couple of miles or so after leaving Halifax, and pass through fishing country down to the shore, which is all rounded, solid rock crawling with artists in summer, and no wonder, and a series of atomic-bomb blasts when the ocean is rough and doing its level best to crush in the shore. Everything is fishing and fishing folk down there. The panorama of homes is a fishing miniature set down on the rocks, as briny as a can of sardines and not much bigger. In the middle of all the lights and shadows is a lip of water on which ride fishing hulls, and you will feel, when you go there, that you are stepping into an oil painting just as it comes into being. Ten minutes away from the lighthouse there is Sunnyside Cottage, where (rooms only) one may stay for $1.00 a day. Farther away and more comfortable is Garrison House, at $2.50 a day.

From Peggy's Cove it is seventeen miles back to Route 3, but first one goes through Glen Margaret, where an ironrock tombstone, Glen Margaret's first, records the death in 1789 of Janette McDonald, who was buried in the sheets her family had treasured since Bonnie Prince Charlie slept in them while in hiding back in Scotland. At Hubbards, which is next, if you talk to any fishermen named Cleveland you may be interested to learn they are descendants of a brother of Grover Cleveland, once President of the United States.

But you may encounter relatives of much more recent American Presidents in the next interesting town, Chester, once a sanctuary for pirates and now "that other Eden" for economic royalists of our nation. It is a little Newport, with an almost perfect yachting course, an island in the bay for every day in the year, and gold, reputedly, buried on one of them: Oak Island. As befits one of the most popular summer resorts in Canada, Chester, only about fifty miles from Halifax (the train takes three hours to make it, though), has a number of fine places in which to stay. The Lovett House, around 110 years old, is perhaps the best, but the Hackmatack (what's in a name?) Inn is good, and there are a number of fine cottages, private homes, and fishing camps, some of them featuring private waterfronts. Chester, from tiptop golf course to a special type of scallops, is outstanding.

At Gold River, between Chester and Mahone Bay, the French settlers are said to have discovered that famous Fort Knox mineral, which the natives are panning out of the tourists these days. Mahone Bay is like Chester all over again, but without plush. A Captain Ephraim Cook, who founded the place in 1754, brought a fort with him on the ship, timbers fitted like a giant Tinker Toy. Bringing logs to Canada is like taking a chorus girl to a Billy Rose night club. There's a local legend that every June 27 you can see a ship blow up and burn at night out in the bay. For June 27 is the anniversary of the date in 1813 when the American privateersman *Young Teazer,* chased into Mahone Harbor by a British man-of-war, was blown up by a British deserter on board who knew he'd be hanged if captured. This spot could use another hotel or two.

Lunenburg, which is next, is a little larger. It is a great big hunk of Germany which you can like. There are all sorts of superlatives you can set down about Lunenburg, such as that it is the home of the greatest deep-sea fishing fleet in America. It is an excellent place from which to set out for the tuna championship of the world, and that's a tip, but the place is, as Bing Crosby would put it, loaded. The famous *Bluenose,* undefeated champion of the North Atlantic fleet, claims it as home port, and that sets the pace for fishermen. Here are almost perfect open docks, where you may walk and inspect the fleet. At sunset you know why the song writer slipped into a rhapsody about red sails. The Bluenose Lodge and the Boscawen are comfortable and several other hotels and private houses are adequate.

You head straight west, inland, for Bridgewater, which

sits amidst the pines on commanding hills overlooking the La Have River, which you cross. This is one of the finest salmon streams in the province. There are boating, swimming, golf, and a museum to help while away the time. At the mouth of the river, not far away by motor, Sieur Pierre du Guast de Monts first touched land, in 1604. A tiny fort here marked the first capital of the province. Mill Village boasts fine fishing and good tourist courts, making it an ideal spot for a camp. At Brooklyn, which is next, you may see the New York newspapers— months before they're printed, because that's the home of the Mersey Paper Company, which specializes in pulp for the big town.

· 2 ·

Pirates and Privateersmen

AFTER SKIRTING Liverpool Bay you are in the home town of the most famous marine fighters ever to live on this continent: the Liverpool privateers—men of 1800 and 1812, who captured a hundred American ships and even made Commando raids on the New England coast. But perhaps even that isn't so spectacular (considering that many an American raid of a similar nature took place) as the fact that these bold sailorfolk went into Massachusetts Bay and cut American ships out from their anchorage. When England was fighting nearly half the world, ships from this one town had the effect of almost another navy. They lay in wait for Frenchmen, Spaniards, Dutchmen, and Yankees. And since the King had mailed them a letter of marque it was all quite legal and many a great family fortune got its start. On the other hand, Americans did the same thing, but no one other community ever did so much with this polite highwayman-of-the-sea business as Liverpool. You may stroll around today and see where these burly boys lived, sawed timbers for their famous craft, drank at the taverns, and manned the guns of Fort Morris which were bombarded by the French and overwhelmed by the Yanks. Thomas H. Raddall has written well in "The Saga of the Rover":

Come gather round the capstan, lads, an' lend an ear to me,
For I've a tale o' the days o' sail, when England won the sea:
Of loss an' gain on the Spanish Main, o' powder, beef an' beer;
O' fightin' Alex Godfrey an' the Rover Privateer.

The Rover's guns may be among those planted on the Liverpool street corners, Nova Scotians leaning on them to the last.

A 956-pound bluefin tuna fish, the largest ever brought to gaff by rod and line, was taken at Liverpool Harbor. Near by are four fine sand beaches. There is excellent canoeing in lakes and streams. The finest place at which to stay in this locality is White Point Beach Lodge, a short distance farther on, although Liverpool offers the Mersey Hotel.

Port Mouton is notable for its name, which it got because a sheep fell off the deck of De Monts' boat on the original exploration. It also merits attention because privateersmen used to lie in wait in the harbor to nab merchantmen headed for Boston, and because it has such fine white beaches and is an idyllic, quiet little place, where good sea food is served. They play golf with red balls against the white sand at the Wobamkek Beach Club, where your putts almost merge with those of the motorboats.

You skim through Port Joli, which means "Beautiful" to the French (but *they* called it Port Noir) and go on to the one-mile cutoff to Lockeport, which is situated on an island, has a beautiful crescent beach, and is famous because the women of the place in 1778 fired muskets and pointed brooms at an American privateer, which hastily jammed on sail and blew. From Lockeport you front Jordan Bay, where Zane Grey caught blue tuna, big as baby elephants. So you swing around this wonderful harbor, one of the best in the world, into Shelburne, where at one time the entire population was honored for disloyalty to the United States. For these people, Americans who wished to remain under the British Crown at the close of the American Revolution, were entitled to place the letters

"U.E.L." (for United Empire Loyalist) after their names.
Descendants of these people even today regard themselves
as heroic because of this historical runout powder. Shelburne is known as a place of quiet charm and a cradle for
famous yachts. Atlantic House and the Souriquois Lake
Cabins are recommended, except for the latter's choice of
a name. When the class-conscious U.E.L.s moved to Shelburne, they established a separate community, Birch-
town, for the thousand or more black slaves they brought
with them. One scrammee alone brought fifty-five. Many
of their descendants are still living in the little place today.

You go on through wood and barren lands across the
short Baccaro Peninsula (the name means "codfish" in
Basque and was once applied to Canada itself) to Upper
and Middle Clyde, where many of the small homes now
belong to American hunters and fishermen. A ten-mile
side trip here brings you to Port La Tour, where, 321
years ago, Charles la Tour built a fort on the sands of
Barrington Bay. A cairn here tells part of the fabulous
La Tour story, made to order for Hollywood except it's
too good.

Claude la Tour brought his son Charles to Acadia about
1609. Charles was left substantial holdings by Biencourt,
and leaving his father at Port Royal, established this fort.
War broke out between France and England (an old, established custom) and Claude la Tour, en route to France,
was one of those captured by a British fleet. Taken to
England, he so charmed the King that he was allowed to
marry one of the Queen's maids of honor, was created a
baronet of Nova Scotia, and given the land between
Lunenburg and Yarmouth. Returning, he tried to get his
son Charles to surrender the Barrington Bay fort. Charles
refused. Claude went back to Port Royal, but when Acadia

was returned to France at the next royal whim, Claude had to flee for safety to his son.

Charles la Tour claimed independence from the auto-cratic rule of D'Aulnay Charnisay, who muscled in when the bona fide agent of the Company of New France died. Charnisay trumped up charges against La Tour, and obtained an order summoning him back to France. La Tour wouldn't go. Charnisay went back and got five hundred soldiers with which to enforce orders. La Tour's pals sent him 150, but Charnisay blocked the harbor and they couldn't land; La Tour went to Boston, secured four ships and 140 men, and with them routed Charnisay and pursued him to Port Royal. Now Charnisay and La Tour's wife ran a race to see who could get to France first and put in a rap against the other. Charnisay tried to have Madame la Tour arrested for treason, but she escaped to England, and returned to Canada. Charnisay waited until La Tour was away from home and the garrison was weak, attacked, won the surrender of the fort, then treacherously hanged the gallant defenders. Madame la Tour died of the shock. Then Charnisay fell out of a boat into the chilly Annap-olis and died of exposure. Madame la Tour having also died, La Tour married Charnisay's widow.

Any decent plot would end there. But, no. Oliver Crom-well put four ships of war at the disposal of New Eng-landers, who recruited five hundred men to attack the Dutch colony at New Amsterdam, later called New York. When peace inopportunely broke out, the New England-ers needed someone to fight, so, despite there being no war with France, they decided not to wait for European intrigue to bring one about and, perhaps out of force of habit, went up and slapped the French around at both Port Royal and La Tour.

So both places again became British. But Charles la
Tour, following in his father's facile footsteps, went over
and charmed the stern Oliver Cromwell into giving him
nearly all of Acadia back again. And he did it with the
argument that he had inherited the baronetcy granted his
father, that same grant he had refused when his father
asked him to surrender the fort on the Barrington sands!
Then, having played out three acts of swell historical
drama, he closed on a good, sound financial note. He sold
his rights and retired to some place where he wouldn't
have to be combing all those damned Indians and colonists out of his carefully coiffured and perfumed locks. Today, near the site of his adventure, there is an apple tree
two hundred years old, but still bearing fruit, and a well
which gives sweet water after almost two centuries.

The small town of Barrington Passage is the shore home
of sailors who work on the yachts of the rich. At Shag
Harbor you are on the extreme southwestern point of
Nova Scotia, and at a house near the post office you can
see chairs made out of materials from famous shipwrecks.
In the Pubnicos, which come next, you have the oldest
Acadian settlements. The Argyles are named after the
western Scottish highlands, which they resemble. Another
short drive past Tusket, where some of the largest Nova
Scotian merchantmen were built and launched, and you
are in Yarmouth, 226.6 miles from Halifax, and the sea
gateway to Nova Scotia. The boats from Boston call here.

Yarmouth is a small city with an excellent library, in
front of which lies the famous Runic Stone, which sup-
posedly proves, or helps to prove, that Norsemen came to
Nova Scotia. The Lakeside Inn is the finest place to stay,
being designed like an English inn of the Elizabethan
age, and you expect to find Errol Flynn strolling about
with leather jerkin and bow and arrow. The Grand Hotel

is more reasonably priced ($5.00 to $7.00 per day), and there are ten to fifteen moderate and really low-priced hostelries, homes, and camps, of which the Snackerie cabins, just outside of town on Route 1, looked best.

Leaving Yarmouth, we let the clutch out on Route 1, taking the principal cities and villages up in order. Hebron is Hebrew for "Friendship," and we enter a friendly dairying country. Three miles off to the right is a small community founded by a couple of gents who wanted to go to Ohio, stopped here, and gave the place the name "Ohio" as a consolation prize. Farther a few miles on this cutoff is Kemptville, a name synonymous with big game. Port Maitland has a fine shore-fishing fleet and many draft oxen, which, of course, will have taken a number of your films by now. While you are some miles from the setting of the famous poem, the area you now enter is thickest today with descendants of Evangeline's people. Select your own candidate for Evangeline and ask to take her photograph. These are plain but wonderful people.

Salmon River isn't so much known for salmon as for blueberries, which are shipped to Boston and there called "Boston blueberries." You probably can snap a ship in the course of construction outdoors at Meteghan. Church Point has the largest wooden church in Canada and Grosses Coques the largest clams on the American coast. At Weymouth I had hoped to discover something which would tie the place to the family of Lord Weymouth, one of the most delightful characters I met in World War II. But all I could learn was that the name came from Weymouth, Massachusetts.

Digby, one of the swankier vacation spots, is a mile or so off Route 1, overlooking Annapolis Basin and facing the Digby Gut, which the politer guidebooks call "The Gap." It is only forty-three miles by boat to St. John, New

Brunswick, and many Americans drive there, then put
their cars on the boat, at from $12 to $18 the round trip,
depending upon whether you brought the runabout or
the long car with which you impress the neighbors. The
place has all the conventional resort attractions, plus clam-
bakes. The Digby scallop fleet is the world's largest. Digby
Pines is complete as a hotel and yet informal and able to
boast of a sylvan setting. And as these things go, the rates
aren't exceptionally high: $10 a day, plus $3.75 for meals.
Also there are Myrtle House ($4.00, American plan), Silver
Glades Inn, Tea Cup Inn, the Salvia, the Scotia, Rambler's
Rest, Digby Gap Inn, and others. At Smith's Cove, in the
same area, there are Harbor View House, Mountain Gap
Inn and Out-of-the-Way Inn, where rates are low and life
is placid.

If you are touring during the third week of July, turn
off four miles to Bear River, where they have an annual
cherry festival, and where, at any time, you may talk to
Indian chieftains of the Micmacs. But if you've seen your
quota of Indians and cherries, continue into the picture-
book Annapolis Valley, famous for apples. Deep Brook's
Colonial Arms, operated by Major and Mrs. W. R. Pell,
has just about everything: private beach, clam digging,
tennis, croquet, and hiking on their own preserves. Modern cottages for housekeeping, with two-bed rooms, were
only $21 a week as they started into the 1948 season. At
Clementsport I heard about Lenley Shaw, who is ninety-
four and gave up the regional fancy-skating championship
two years ago, so the young folks could have a chance. I
didn't get to see him: he was fixing the foundation of his
house, lying flat on his back in the mud. He hopes to
continue as a professional hunting guide until he is at
least a hundred. Here, too, I was told about Jack Durland,
the Nova Scotian Fred Allen, who never smiled as he told

stories which were famous all the way to "the Boston States."

Annapolis Royal was formerly Port Royal, whence Charnisay sailed out to further his feuding with La Tour. The place has been attacked or undergone siege a score of times and been sacked four or five times, twice by pirates. Fort Anne Historic Park tells you the historical story and it might be interesting to recall that *Quietly My Captain Waits,* a best seller by a feminine author, had as its setting the old French fort. Here in Annapolis Royal is the very old, interestingly old, Hillsdale House (with board, from $5.00 to $7.00 a day), where at least one British king has stayed. You must leave Route 1 to get to Lower Granville, the oldest permanent white settlement north of the Gulf of Mexico. Just as it looked 343 years ago, the Original Champlain Habitation has been copied. This is where they originated that unique club you have heard so much about ever since you entered Nova Scotia: the Order of the Good Time (or Cheer). To while away the evenings the members took turns being host, buying game, supplying wines, and drinks with more authority.

Passing Mochelle (note the dikes filled with water), Round Hill, Tupperville (behind the village, the waterfalls), Bridgetown, which got its name when suggested by a pretty girl at a town dinner, and the extravagantly named town of Paradise, you come to Lawrencetown, where sportsmen congregate to whip the Annapolis River for salmon. Here, and at Middleton and Wilmot, United Empire Loyalists flocked as the British evacuated New York, among them descendants of John Alden and Priscilla Mullins, two hundred Harvard graduates, and the Chief Justice of Massachusetts. Off Route 1 seven miles is Margaretsville, scene of a classical story of retribution rivaling anything in the Bible. On Christmas Eve, 1793,

Peter Barnes hung beacons on fir trees and lured the *Saucy Nancy* to her doom on the rocks, a bit of calculated horseplay much more prevalent than nonsailors might believe. Then, exactly twenty years later, again on Christmas Eve, Barnes had done the taverns in Middleton and was returning home to his lone cabin. Taking a bearing on the lantern a farmer had left outside his barn, the culprit fell over the cliff to his doom on the very rocks which had killed the crew of the *Saucy Nancy!*

The ribbon of Route 1 unwinds for miles through fruit land, with maple shade trees over the highway and country churches here and there to give the scene romance. Some of them are very old, like St. Mary's at Aylesford. At Kentville, named after the fat Georgian who built all the forts, they put on the Nova Scotia Apple Blossom Festival, complete with queens and press agents. Here the Cornwallis Inn is heartily recommended. Just off the main road near here is Upper Dyke Village, birthplace of the Fuller Brush Man, Alfred Fuller, history's second most impressive success with the phrase, "Go out on the highways and byways . . ." and the man who caused the launching of a thousand quips. Hall Harbor, at the end of this same secondary road, was the scene of a pirate landing in a heavy fog, when the villagers, tired of being pillaged, circled the cutthroats, killed their guards, swiped their gold, and buried it on the beach. For years, so the story goes, none of the good burghers wished to use this tainted money. They forgot where they buried it. Now their great grandchildren haven't any qualms; they just can't find the filthy stuff.

A side trip from Greenwich (named after the observatory town in England) takes you to the Lookoff, a magnificent view of the Minas Basin and six river valleys. On the way out to the Lookoff is a "Magnetic Hill," where you'll swear your car will roll backward up a rather steep grade, with the motor off.

Wolfville is known as the center of the Land of Evangeline and many visitors make their headquarters there, although I found no place equipped with enough plumbing for all its guests. The Hotel Paramount, Harris Cabins, and Evangeline Beach Hotel and Cabins are comfortable to passable. In Grand Pré there'll be hushed groups treading through the flower gardens and looking up at the statue of Evangeline at the Dominion Atlantic Railway's Memorial Park. The pulling power of one great poem brought them all there. And while in Grand Pré don't fail to see the Church of the Covenanters.

Hantsport wasn't content to send her men and ships on the seven seas; one of them, Buckman Pasha, became High Admiral of the Turkish Fleet. You pass on through Falmouth to Windsor, where the tides vary forty feet. There is a golf course here which has the moat of an old fort as a hazard on green number seven. Here in Windsor lived Judge Thomas Chandler Haliburton, the writer who dreamed up Sam Slick. His former home is now a museum. But if you ask natives of Windsor what the town is known for they'll tell you: "Windsor has the oldest permanent fair in America; you oughta see our cheeses."

At Bedford, Route 1 joins Route 2, which you now take to Truro. There you branch off on Route 4 so as to get over on Cape Breton Island and do the Cabot Trail; then you come back to Truro and wind up other parts of Nova Scotia which can safely and comfortably be reached by automobile —if there's any particular reason for doing it.

Through Waverley, which got its name from the Waverley Novels, to Wellington, called after the Iron Duke (although they will extend you the warm hand of welcome), to Grand Lake, which is well along as a planned fishing resort, and

then you come to Enfield. Enfield was the home of Edward
Horne, the prospector who found the great Noranda gold
mines of northern Quebec, seventy-five miles from the end
of steel; then someone discovered gold near his own home
town. The old *Acres of Diamonds* theme again.

The Place Where Ground Nuts Grow is on your map as
Shubenacadie, where there is a large Indian residential
school. "Stewiacke" is mixed Micmac for "Flowing Softly
From Still Water," and when the basic place-names society
gets around to it they'll probably call it "Seeping." So on
to Truro, truly called the Hub of Nova Scotia. While I was
doing the province it seemed as though every time I looked
up I was back at Truro. And as might be expected at such
a traffic center, there are a number of good places to stay.
Among others there are the Scotia Hotel, Open Kitchen
Guest House, Stanley Hotel, Maritime Tourist Cabins, and
Truro Over-Nite Cabins. From here we take Route 6 to
Hawkesbury, 115 miles away. Turn left on Walker Street
and cross Salmon River bridge, continue through Kemp-
town, named after one of Wellington's officers, Sir James
Kempt (but the canny Scotch dropped that extra "t"), and
you are soon in Pictou County, famed for agriculture, mining, and the number of illustrious politicans and educators
it has supplied both Canada and the United States. First
town is Salt Springs, and then off the road six miles, Mill
Brook, which was once called Bear Brook because the natives, long before electric lights, couldn't go out at night
without tipping their hats to, or shaking hands with, a
bear. The legend is that too many of them resembled substantial matrons of the area, after dark.

West River is small but interesting. Here's where they
started the West River Farming Society, embodying in the
rules a fine of five shillings for cursing (or swearing, either,
so they said); or for changing the subject; or use of any in-

decent language. Each member had to attend meetings armed with an essay or oral presentation on an announced agricultural subject. First topic was: What is the best method of preparing and increasing manure? There is no record of how many members were fined.

At Alma, Route 6 branches off to Pictou, where a young British acquaintance I met on the train was sailing back to England. The Master of the ship, in ill humor, perhaps because Britain's Socialist Government planners had changed ports and cargo for the trip on several occasions, was allowing no liquor on board for anyone other than himself. I smuggled a quart of gin to my friend and, chances are, got more of a glow out of that than he did drinking it.

Westville and Stellarton are mining towns. Then you come to New Glasgow, where prosperity is founded on the solid coal seam. Here I was met by Elliot Sutherland, and his red-haired and sparklingly pretty wife. Elliot, editor of the *New Glasgow News,* "watched out for" the combined world press on the King and Queen's visit to that section of Canada; so I'd heard of him before. He and his wife took me into their home and plied me with food, wine, and anecdotes. They told me that there are so many Scotsmen in this area, and owing to the Scot's paucity of given names, many a MacDonald had to be known as Black John, or Tuppence Johnny, or Wild Angus to differentiate. But I believe the best illustration of these names is to be found in Duncan's *Here's To Canada.* "And now children," a primary grade teacher said, according to Miss Duncan, "have I made it clear why animals are called quadrupeds and men are called bipeds? Willy ... what is it that a man has two of and a cow has four?" And, Miss Duncan explains, that's why one little boy answered, all through life, to the name of Willy Teats.

We drove out to the pleasant beach facing Northumberland Strait, and Elliot told me discovery of coal was the genesis of New Glasgow; that nearly all the first diggers settling along the East River were bachelors. "Three of them, hearing of an immigrant ship which was to arrive at Halifax, walked over there and as soon as the gangplank was down, walked up and down the decks proposing to the ladies of their sudden choice," Elliot said. "They quickly found them, were married then and there, and walked back the next day. Which is considered sufficient answer to the question: What's time to a Scotsman?"

We got so busy talking, these charming people and I, that you'll have to take Joseph Howe's word for it that the view from Fraser's Mountain "surpasses that of any other province." There was, of course, no way of foreseeing it, but I was to meet the Sutherlands again out on the West Coast, farther away from their home than their ancestors had come from Scotland. (Hotels in New Glasgow: Norfolk, Fraser, Scotian, Parker House, Westhaven; but if you're driving, Pine Grove Cabins, Routes 4 and 6.)

At Barney's River, named after Barney McGee, an Ulsterman who came there in 1776, one of Elliot Sutherland's relatives, was an early settler. John Sutherland, a hearty Highlander, wore kilts and neither inclement weather nor ridicule could ever get him to wear pants. He lived to a rewarding old age and was buried in kilts.

Antigonish, Scottish to its last sporran, sounds as though it were straight from the bonny braes. But the word is Micmac, and means "Where Branches Are Broken by Bears Getting Beechnuts." There is a vital experiment going on in Antigonish. The co-operative movement is gaining new impetus, new experimentation, through the University of St. Francis Xavier, Roman Catholic institution. People are being taught to produce, as a group, the goods which are best suited for production in that locality. Then, after production by basic groups, buying and selling is done by groups, with group financing. In a world beset by Communism and wild-eyed Socialism, this co-op way may come to be important among democratic peoples who intend to stay democratic. Establishment of a credit union, or group savings and loan bank, is the first step in any community. I recall how sensible this all sounded then and now, and how my own home town, Laredo, Texas, could use a large measure of all this—particularly co-operative banking. (In Antigonish, the Royal George Hotel, with food and lodging generally very reasonable.)

Bayfield Road next, small but growing as a holiday resort, and Tracadie, or camping ground, then Monastery Harbor au Bouche and Auld's Cove (both fishing settlements), and thence to Mulgrave, where there is a twenty-four-hour ferry service to Port Hawkesbury, in Cape Breton. If you go over in "civilized" hours, 6 A.M. to midnight, the price is $1.00 for motor car and driver, 15 cents for passengers. After that the toll doubles. Trailers, 25 cents; big trailers, 50 cents.

It's a big ride for the money: nearly a mile. The Strait of Canso is about thirteen miles long and joins the Gulf of St. Lawrence with the Atlantic Ocean. The theory is that at one time Cape Breton Island was a part of the mainland. But by being cut off from that mainland, it somehow seemed a great deal more remote than it actually was, and the picture grew up of a romantic green hell grasping shimmering salt lakes.

History followed legend, and now the romance, history, and legend have merged. But certainly Cape Breton Island is as interesting physically, in its northern way, as the most pleasing South Sea island could ever be if its tropical luxuriance were ideal. Cape Breton undoubtedly was visited by the Norsemen, and one wonders why all the hoopla about Columbus when it has been pretty definitely established that fishermen were making annual visits to the great banks around Cape Breton long before Columbus ever practiced his technique on Isabella. When Shakespeare was translating human experience into lasting drama, British, French, Spanish, and Portuguese fishermen knew the Cape Breton harbors.

You'll get your welcome to Port Hawkesbury from a big roof sign. From any of the upper streets there is a comprehensive view of the Straits you have just crossed. Now head left and seek out Route 5 to Port Hastings, and on to Whycocomagh set among the mountains and deep glens and overlooking the Bras d'Or Lakes (not pronounced "Brass Door" but "Bra-door," from the French, meaning "Arms of Gold"). You skirt St. Patrick Channel for miles going to Baddeck, a village so peaceful and wonderful it is like a perfect day remembered out of a sunny childhood. This place was made famous by C. Dudley Warner's book, *Baddeck and That Sort of Thing,* and afterward was "discovered" by many famous people, including A. Graham Bell. Mr. Bell was made so famous by inventions that he was impersonated by Don Ameche, final accolade in the United States. Bell's grave is on his former estate, Beinn Bhreagh, Gaelic for "Beautiful Hill," which is three miles off Route 5. Rather than try to visit his tomb you would do better to pause and drink in the beauties of the countryside he loved, something which will bring you closer to this great man.

Baddeck was the scene of the building and flying of the first airplane of the British Empire. It is the beginning and the end of the Cabot Trail.

THE CABOT TRAIL

There are at least as many different opinions about this trip as miles of travel (185). But you shouldn't start out unless you have heard the word that it "likely won't rain," because the road is not paved, there are boggy places during any storm, and some potholes any time, so keep your speed down. Carry ice water, cameras, spare tires, and at least one back-seat driver to tell you to slow down and to get scared now and then. I'd advise going clockwise because that way you have the inside of the road and, just at the right time, the sun is at your back, which as you know works wonders for sightseeing, just as it does for snapshots. And it would be well to take two days on the trip, stopping at the excellent Keltic Lodge, near Ingonish. This leaves you only sixty or so miles to go on the second day—a mighty fine feeling. Whenever anyone passes you, stop the car and allow the dust to settle on the trail ahead of you. You can start any time in the day, for no matter how early you wish to start, there'll probably be some determined American ahead of you.

Now just a word about the villages you'll see on the way: From Margaree Harbor to Cap Rouge the natives are "Acadians," speak French, and are "quaint." Friar's Head gets its name from a huge boulder, resembling a friar's cowl. During rough weather it "snows" spume along the road. Cheticamp Village has an excellent harbor where you may pick up guides and boats for fishing. The church here is interesting and open for inspection. Just six miles from the village the trail enters Cape Breton Highlands National Park, with its exciting hills, highest in the Maritimes. This is no time to be a Barney Oldfield! Next is Pleasant Bay, once called Grand Tosh Bay, and still earlier, Grand Anse Bay; and until 1927 there is no telling what it was called by people who could only get to it by boat or by a narrow footpath through the mountains. In winter this village is frozen in and the mailman mushes the *postales* with a dog team. Not far from this hamlet is one of the more breath-taking views: that from the top of Big Intervale.

North Ingonish and its highland parapets, nature's best, will alert you to the beauties to be found in hiking this area from South Ingonish, where Keltic Lodge offers comfort, tennis, golf, and the means to go swordfishing. Below Cape Smoky, imposing headland often split by fleecy clouds, there is another "Magnetic Hill." Now you drift through a number of small fishing villages which distill enchantment and you come to St. Ann, scene of a remarkable exodus to New Zealand about ninety years ago. Half the town picked up belongings, built ships and sailed away "Down Under." Stop at the schoolhouse here and ask to listen to class. The work goes on in Gaelic (it's the only class conducted in that language in North America), and you'll be welcome. An exhibition of implements and utensils used by early Scottish settlers is here for your edification. And so back through the Glen Tosh area to Baddeck.

A glance at the map will show that Route 5, from Baddeck, will take you down to Sydney, but that, once there, it would be better to return via Route 4, which is well paved. Sydney, founded by a former mayor of Albany, New York, has one of the finest harbors in the world, nearer to Great Britain than any other American mainland port and six hundred miles nearer to Rio de Janeiro (it will amaze you, this geography!) than is New York. Here in an ancient Anglican Church, St. George's, is a chair from the wardroom of Admiral Lord Nelson in the *Victory,* presented by the Admiral himself. Among the city's other attractions are ducks and geese at Wentworth Park. You may pet them, if you go around petting ducks and geese. Sydney's mines are formidable and imposing, but there isn't much chance you're interested. (Best places to stay in Sydney: Isle Royal at $2.50 a day, up; the Vidal, the Nova, the Cliefden House, the MacKenzie House, the Sydney River Overnight Cabins, and Lakeview Cabins.)

Take Highway 22 out George Street, for a visit to Louisburg, where the French built an "impregnable" fortress costing millions to "control" the mouth of the St. Lawrence River, only to have it fall and fall and fall. New England soldiers stormed this forest Maginot Line.

There isn't much to be seen on Route 4, returning, until you get to St. Peter's. Here Nicholas Denys, of France, worked hard and experienced travail rivaling that of Job. The foundations of his fort may still be seen. Denys also founded Guysboro, in the county of the same name, which you may visit by returning to the mainland and turning left off Route 4 onto Route 16. Guysboro, at the head of Chedabucto Bay, is a restful town where you may spend a few hours around and about the ruins of old Fort St. Louis. (Grant's Hotel, very reasonable.)

Except for a trip over Route 2 to Parrsboro, located on the northern shore of Minas Basin, further motoring in Nova Scotia must await projected road building. (In Parrsboro: the Ottawa House By the Sea, Cumberland Hotel, Parrsboro Hotel, and Riverview Cabins are recommended, with rates medium to low, for these times.) A local legend recounts how two centuries ago an Italian pirate captured a British ship and killed everyone aboard except the captain's beautiful daughter. A storm having driven the pirate ship to a landing at Black Point, near Parrsboro, the buccaneer tried to subdue the maiden, but failed, so put her in a cave and sealed it. Then the crew picked up "a treasure" of amethysts lying on the beach and sailed away. The heroine perished, and with her died the secret of how a girl can resist rape even when confronted by troops of bloodthirsty murderers; an important formula, seeing how many rape cases we have today. Anyway, they say this maiden's shrieks can still be heard from the cave, on certain nights; perhaps she's still trying to get her message out to anxious femininity.

So, on a note of hope, we head toward New Brunswick.

· 3 ·

Habit-forming New Brunswick

NEW BRUNSWICK is Sherwood Forest in a young man's dream, plus some modern habitations and conveniences.

The trees, fish, game, and satisfying solitude to be found in New Brunswick today were common to the remainder of the northern half of the continent a hundred years ago. So-called "progress" having passed New Brunswick by, as commercial development goes, the province is now profiting from presenting a wild-life picture as good as that of a century ago, plus some fishing unique on the globe at any time. Oh, it also has some natural phenomena worth seeing, interesting views, historical spots, wonderful sea food, better-than-ordinary beaches, and native handicrafts worth buying. But New Brunswick is habit-forming because of its remarkable rivers, its great sweeps of second-growth but never second-rate timber; because its bear stories are not only fabulous, they're true and can yet be topped by another season's crop; and because there's no thrill to a sportsman like luring, snaring, and taking New Brunswick's special types of fish which, besides fighting virtues, have the ability to keep right on growing in the imagination and in the telling many months after their violent demise.

New Brunswick is not as old nor as permanently old-looking as Quebec, nor nearly as foreign; it is not as salty as Nova Scotia; it is not as well cultivated as Prince Edward Island (85 per cent of it is not cultivated at all, unless harvesting wood pulp amounts to cultivation). but it is the best-watered area in the world. Otherwise it is miles and miles of trees, with here and there a black shanty in the woods or an unpainted village which is a springboard to the bush. Guides live in these small towns during the winter, or their wives do, and they go forth again to cut trees. They have this forested Shangri-la divided up among themselves in the same way that a manufacturer might divide the United States among his traveling salesmen, and there must, by law, be a guide with every nonresident hunter (except when hunting birds, when two hunters may "divide" a guide between them). Many New Brunswick crown waters formerly under lease are now open to fishing under an angling license, but since these matters vary from season to season, and it is legal to fish in parts of certain streams but not others, all of this being detailed and involved, we refer you to the New Brunswick Government Bureau of Information, Fredericton, New Brunswick, which upon request will mail you a folder on the game laws, and information about guides.

Unlike the New Brunswick Bureau of Information, which is definitely awake and on the *qui vive,* the province on the map looks like a hibernating bear, particularly if you will draw a circle around the "eyes" at Bathurst. This bear has its back to the state of Maine, it is juggling Miscou Island on its nose, while its feet, in profile, are resting on the solid rock of Nova Scotia and its hind quarters are settling gingerly into the turbulent waters of the Bay of Fundy. Fittingly, its spinal column is the St. John River, often described as Canada's Rhine; but if the Chamber of Commerce down there objects to what all this makes of St. John, let them know that this is merely an old bear's tale, and I really don't think that of them at all; I really *liked* St. John, even if it was almost dirty enough to make apt the implied characterization.

New Brunswick is just a dry remark or two short of the size of Maine, or nearly 28,000 square miles. It has many miles of paved highways well situated to let the tourists in, from Maine, Quebec, and Nova Scotia; to serve the principal cities, get the people to the beaches, and give the sportsman a run, rill, or river for his money. You will have discovered that motoring in Canada costs about $10 a day for a single person (or a married person traveling alone, for that matter), or about $16 a day for two persons who can share the same double bed. Of course prices vary and fluctuate, and as a matter of fact, nothing seems permanent in Canada any more since even Mr. King has retired, having lasted as premier no longer than the memory of living man. Motoring costs may be slightly less than the above amount in New Brunswick, but the accommodations will not always be as satisfactory.

Trains and buses run in from Boston, New York, Montreal, and Quebec, and from Halifax the Canadian Pacific Railway, via Annapolis Valley, and the Canadian National Railways, via Truro, Sackville, and Moncton, bring you in. There are sailings from Boston, New York, Digby, Nova Scotia (to St. John), and from Prince Edward Island, as has been previously noted. By air there are connections from Montreal (and the west), New York, Boston (through both Moncton and St. John), and from Halifax. Many sportsmen fly in for the week end, for frenetic fishing, whipping the streams and themselves into a lather and departing for their plush-lined treadmills in New York with ice-packed catches costing cool thousands. From Nova Scotia the motorist would take Route 2 from Amherst to Sackville (which would be the logical place to start this gadding about New Brunswick, since we have already done Nova Scotia; but we will enter from Maine, since most American tourists will have done so). From the Province of Quebec, along beautiful Matapedia River Valley, through Camp-bellton, and Highway Number 2 from Rivière du Loup, Quebec, through Edmundston, which is, by the way, 90 per cent French-Canadian. From New York and Boston, take Route 1, via New Haven, Boston, Portland, Bangor, and the junction of Routes 1 and 2, leading to whatever entry point desired. There are the following possibilities:

Through Van Buren, Maine, on U.S. Route 1 (the New Brunswick town of St. Leonards across a short bridge, on Canadian Highway Number 2; by way of Fort Fairfield, Maine, on U.S. Route 16) the nearest New Brunswick town being Andover, on Route 2; via Houlton, Maine, on U.S. Route 2, to Woodstock, New Brunswick, on Trans-Canada Route 2; driving through Vanceboro, Maine, on U.S. Route 16, to McAdam, New Brunswick (the connect-ing road between Vanceboro and Trans-Canada Highway Number 2 is supposed to be paved by the time you can read this; it is to connect with Route 2 at Long Creek, eighteen miles from the provincial capital, Fredericton); and, finally, by way of those internationally famous sister cities, Calais, Maine, and St. Stephen, New Brunswick. Calais is on U. S. Route 1 and St. Stephen, which leads the way to St. John, the largest city in New Brunswick, is on Route 1.

Now let us examine the roads. Trans-Canada Highway Route 2, extending from the boundary of the Province of Quebec to the Nova Scotian line, 410 miles, is very good. The scenery is unexcelled, 267 of the miles paralleling the beautiful St. John River. To check on this Trans-Canada Highway was one of my more important objectives. But I soon discovered it isn't like a federal highway in the United States; that it is under provincial control, is of varying widths and stages of completion—merely a "desig-nated" road, sometimes because it is the only lateral one heading in the general direction of the coast. The Trans-Canada really started back at Halifax or Sydney, went on to Truro and Amherst in Nova Scotia; Moncton, Saint John, Fredericton and Edmundston in New Brunswick; Rivière du Loup, Quebec, and Montreal in Quebec; Ottawa, North Bay, Cochrane, Port Arthur, and Kenora in Ontario; Winnipeg and Brandon in Manitoba; Regina and Moose Jaw in Saskatchewan; Medicine Hat, Calgary, and Banff in Alberta; and Golden, Revelstoke, Kamloops, Lytton, to Vancouver in British Columbia.

It is a 4,195-mile scenic drive now, passable everywhere but a bit inferior in wet weather on scores of stretches. Driving over it is a wonderful way to see our neighbor to the north. But because of the much wider scope of this book we must take up all the tourist possibilities in each province and move steadily toward the west. After all, Canada has 550,000 miles of roads, 125,000 of them all-weather, and the Trans-Canada Highway is merely one of its more important segments.

Now back to Fredericton, New Brunswick's capital. Using it as traffic center, you can go to Sussex on the way to Moncton across Route 9, Sussex being halfway between St. John and Moncton, with the road not too bad; there is excellent gravel in places, being prepared for paving. From Fredericton to St. Stephen, the road is paved part way; on Route 3 there is a good gravel road to Thomaston (preparatory to paving), and a decent gravel road the remainder of the way.

Here is the summary on the road from Fredericton to the North Shore via Newcastle, Bathurst, Campbellton, on Routes 8 and 11: to Boiestown, fair gravel road being prettied up for paving; Boiestown to Newcastle, paved; Newcastle to Bathurst, smooth sailing, with smooth sliding on the few curves, like any graveled road; and Bathurst to

Huge pulp-log reserve pile destined for paper mill in New Brunswick.

Logs get expert handling as they are sped on their way to the mill.

Rolling surf at New River Beach, along Highway No. 1, in New Brunswick, at a spot about halfway between Saint Stephen and Saint John.

A glimpse of the historic Saint John River and Highway No. 2. This route traverses almost the length of the province of New Brunswick.

New Brunswick Government
Information Bureau Photos

Famed Reversing Falls in the
Saint John River. During part
of day water drops toward sea
and then reverses to drop up-
stream. This is caused by the
ebb and flow of Fundy tides.

Champlain Monument in Saint
John. One of the first of the
French *voyageurs*, Champlain
discovered the Saint John
River. In the statue his arm
points to mouth of the river.

The "Bore" on the Pedicodiac River near Moncton, N. B. Owing to compression of tide, water rolls up river in a wall several feet high.

Magnetic Hill near Moncton amazes visitors by uncanny effect on car.

MAGNETIC HILL
TO APPRECIATE THIS
PHENOMENON PROCEED
TO SPOT INDICATED
BY WHITE POST
TURN OFF MOTOR
RELEASE BRAKES

Known as "Southern Head," this formation is at southernmost tip of Grand Manan, largest of the Fundy Isles off coast of New Brunswick.

Lighthouse called "Swallow Tail Light" marks headland on Grand Manan.

Summer home of the late Franklin D. Roosevelt on Campobello Island.

Campobello Island, smallest of the Fundy Isles, is famous as a summer resort. This is Mallock Beach. Islanders farm and fish.

Lake Utopia as seen through a frame of white birches. Beautiful little lakes like this abound in Charlotte County, New Brunswick.

"The Rocks" at Hopewell Cape in Albert County, New Brunswick. This eccentric rock formation, caused by tides, is a tourist attraction.

Blessing the Fleet is an annual ceremony at Caraquet, New Brunswick. Clerics go out in a small boat to bless North Shore fishing fleet.

Sunset on the fishing fleet at Caraquet. Deep-sea fishing is the traditional occupation of residents of the eastern and northern coasts.

Campbellton, paved. Route 17, between Campbellton and St. Leonard, across the top of the province, is under construction and barely rates a 70, which is just passing.

The Eastern Seaboard: from Moncton, along the coast to Bathurst, Campbellton, and so on, paved *très bien,* and the same for Route 16 from Sackville to Cape Tormentine (where we take the ferry to Prince Edward Island).

Now we will take a quick trip around a few of the better roads, with a dash of comment, here and there, to spice up this Portal to the Maritimes, this Unspoiled Province by the Sea. We enter at St. Stephen–Calais, because the coastal-road traffic is very heavy and the chances are that will coincide with most plans.

If you go to a fire in St. Stephen, New Brunswick, you may see the fire department from Calais, Maine, or vice versa all the way around. And when you take a drink of water in Calais, it has come from St. Stephen's reservoir over in Canada. These two towns have such a fine friendship they've been the subject of a *Saturday Evening Post* story, and in many ways they remind me of what goes on between my home town, Laredo, Texas, and Nuevo Laredo, Tamaulipas, Mexico. The river here, the St. Croix, gets its name because, with its two tributaries, it forms a cross. (In St. Stephen: the Park Hotel, Better Duck In Camps and Wewana Tourist Cabins; and wewanna know where they get those names.)

St. Andrews-by-the-Sea boasts a fairly swanky hotel, the Algonquin (with bath, single, $12 per day, American plan). Here there is everything: fishing, swimming, tennis, golf, bowling, music, and, no doubt, romance. Not quite so swank: the Commodore Hotel ($5.00 per day per person, American plan). Also the Seaside Inn. There are several rather good tourist homes, but one could wish the percentages of baths to the total number of rooms were higher, and this is a wish general to the whole of Canada, not just New Brunswick, and particularly not just St. Andrews-by-the-Sea. St. Andrews looks out on Passama-quoddy Bay, the arm of the Bay of Fundy which separates the extreme eastern coast of Maine from southwestern New Brunswick. From this area you can arrange trips to Grand Manan Island, which is rocky and rugged, and Campobello Island, the restful spot which was the boyhood summer home of President Franklin D. Roosevelt, and often in his wistful, adult thoughts.

Here at St. Andrews I was reminded of the biblical references to Moses leading his people through the divided waters of the Red Sea. For you can actually motor over Baybottom Road to Minister's Island at low tide, while at high the vast waters of Fundy dominate the entire panorama. As you drive along the south shore toward St. John there'll be opportunity to observe the highest, most arrant tides in the world. Powerful, moody, freakish, the Bay-of-Fundy waters are making a certain conquest of inlet and harbor and cliff end. New Brunswick was once merely a county of Nova Scotia, then became a separate province, and now students of Fundy tell us removal of three "trifling" obstacles would allow Fundy's tidal sweep to pour into the Gulf of St. Lawrence, severing New Brunswick and Nova Scotia, to make an island out of the latter. They point out that the highest land on Chignecto's Isthmus is only seventeen feet above the level of the highest tides; that there is, moreover, evidence of coastal sinking in the fact that many rivers flow into estuaries bounded by cliffs, whereas the east coast, for the most part, is low with mosses and marshes.

With perhaps a visit to Lepreau Falls, remaining relic of glacial days, you are soon in St. John, oldest incorporated city in British America. Champlain, as ubiquitous an ex-

plorer as George Washington was a sleeper-outer, even if
all the New Jersey and New York–Long Island signs be
taken at their face value, discovered the St. John River
'way back in 1604. And it was here that La Tour held
forth against Charnisay and finally married the beautiful
widow of his bitter enemy. Here the United Empire Loyalists came in droves, unconvinced that the United States
would be much of a place, what with no king. They laid
the town out in lines as severe and formal as their own
thoughts and the principles which they rigidly adhered to.
And it isn't a pretty place, but the people are pleasant,
there's at least one pretty flower market, a really choice
museum for Canadiana, and Atlantic salmon in the restaurants, finest fish you ever ate, with greens known as
"fiddleheads." These fiddleheads, which you may be served
in spring and early summer, have curled tops which resemble tiny violins, and New Brunswick people tell you
they are found only there, mainly along the St. John River.
New Brunswickers also like dulse, an edible seaweed with
salty tang, but me, I believe you can carry these things
too far.

The chief attraction in this, New Brunswick's principal
metropolis and famous all-weather port, is the reversing
falls or rapids. The river is laced into a 450-foot girdle of
gorges and when the tide is out, trips roaringly over a
twenty-six-foot chasm. But when the tide comes in, this
fills up and the waters of the river are pushed back, "uphill." Boats can get through the gorge at the time when
the two movements seem to have fought each other to a
standstill. It is recorded that the Duke of Kent, the plump
one with a passion for cannon, chronometers, and co-
quettes, took a boat out on the dangerous waters at such a
time. Nowadays small yachts start pleasure trips of scores
of miles on the mighty St. John that same way.

It was an early boat out of St. John that caught the Peabody bird—and named it. Old Captain Sam Peabody used to go upriver every spring to represent the St. John merchants, calling at every landing along the way. At the same period, at the first breakup of the ice, the white-throated sparrow would make its appearance along the stream. Wits linked the two visitors breaking winter's monotony and said the bird was whistling "Old Sam Peabody—Peabody— Peabody." Old Sam has long since gone to his heavenly Hellespont but the bird is still called the Peabody. And out of another age St. John contributed some of the strongest sea sagas, like that of the *Marco Polo,* known as the fastest ship in the world. She was built in Courtney Bay, Saint John, the largest ship of her famous New Brunswick timbers to that time, and won world fame by beating the steamer *Australia* from England to Melbourne. Her skipper, Captain Bully Forbes, who successfully overcame derision by action and good publicity, got a publicist's final reward, favorable mention (and a tieup with the famous Marco Polo) on his tombstone. And by the way, Walter Pidgeon, the movie player, and Louis B. Mayer, who make lots of money in the same business, are from St. John.

"In St. John," say the posters, "everything is cool but the hospitality." There is the Admiral Beatty ($2.20 up, European; $5.50 up, American), and then there are the Royal, White House Lodge, and Balmoral Court, and some other places to stay.

Leaving what the British call "Sinjun" we drive through Hampton on Route 2, down the Pickwaucket Road through historic old Kingston to Moss Glen, following the shores of the scenery-making Kennebecasis River, a drive rating very kind words, indeed. We've come to Moss Glen because of the Dykelands Pottery, home of the gifted artisans, Kjeld and Erica Deichmann. They've set aside Friday for visitors.

Through a charming countryside, after you regain Route 2, you drive to Moncton, second largest city of New Brunswick. Moncton is about what you would expect of a town chiefly noted as a railroad yard and repair and maintenance center. It is called "Hub of the Maritimes," probably because when you get away from there you feel like shouting "Hubba, hubba!" What made the place enjoyable for me was the gracious hospitality of Mr. and Mrs. J. H. Norton (he is traffic manager of the Canadian National Railways there). They took me down to see the "Bore," which amiably performed, but not very spectacularly this time. From a small park in town we watched while the Petitcodiac River changed quickly from an orthodox stream coursing its way through mud flats to a crested, small wall of wetness running the other way. This time it wasn't spectacular but they tell me there are occasions when the "Bore" comes in like a huge breaker. Later we went to the Magnetic Hill and enjoyed ourselves coasting "uphill" with the motor shut off, and listening to comments of the amazed tourists from both the United States and remote parts of Canada. The first explanation offered about this zany creation of nature is that there was magnetic ore in the ground which pulled you uphill. There isn't; it's an optical illusion, but don't let knowing that spoil it for you. Because the danged thing is almost perfect as an illusion. When there's water in the ditch alongside the road you'll swear that's flowing uphill, too. Have fun, kiddies. And I'll wager you never find a perspective where the thing looks natural. "Must have had moose juice on my cereal this morning instead of milk," we overheard one bemused motorist gasp.

Then we motored all around the excellent beaches of Shediac, had lobster, topped off with blueberry pie, at the Bayview Restaurant, near Cocagne and pronounced the meal only sensational. This place is no Waldorf oyster bar; no plush but the real thing: clams and quahaugs. My visit with the Nortons only emphasized a truth we all know: if you can visit with an intelligent family you have a distinct advantage in knowing, and therefore liking, any spot on the globe.

I stayed at the Hotel Brunswick. I am unofficially informed that the railroad which owns this hotel plans to replace it. It is passable, but none too good for a city the size of Moncton, especially in view of its strategic location. There are also the Queen Hotel, and near by, Clearview Cabins and Wilson's Evergreen Cabins.

One of the most pleasurable trips from Moncton is that down Route 2 to Sackville. En route you may turn right at College Bridge to St. Joseph, where in the Convent of Our Lady of the Sacred Heart resident students and housewives of the community are doing something special in hand-weaving. Again, in Sackville, the Art School of Mount Allison University has fostered these basic arts. Attractive tweeds and original patterns for furniture upholstery are featured, but I particularly call your attention to their invention of woven window curtains of transparent wool. At Mount Allison may be found the Owens Museum of Fine Arts with its many treasures in paintings. From Sackville, which is on the Tantramar River at the head of Cumberland Bay, you may drive out to Mount View and get an impression of the great marshes which were diked up by the French settlers long, long ago. You don't have to go to Holland for that sort of thing; they reclaimed fifty square miles and it has been producing a quality hay for seven different generations now.

About seven miles from Sackville watch carefully for the road marker indicating the route to Fort Beausejour. They've marked the fort site well but not the way to get to it. Here the power of the French in Acadia was snatched away by General Monckton of the British Army, leading New England troops. (When they named Moncton after him, a clerk, who must have been a sign painter at heart, left out the "k." Since that time "k-konscious" persons have been agitating for the correct spelling, but the city fathers have adamantly responded: "Don't monkey with [sic] Moncton.")

You are welcome at the Sackville Country Club, for golf, and I found the Silver Lake development at Middle Sackville interesting for boating and bathing; Marshland's Inn was pleasant and good, as was Frosty Hollow Inn, three miles west of Sackville. To "go on the rocks" without going broke, drive across the Petitcodiac River into Albert County on Route 14 to Hopewell Cape, then hunt the sign marked "The Rocks." This takes you to the red sandstone cliffs worn into fantastic shapes by Fundy tides. Time yourself to arrive when they are low and you may explore the caverns. They and the monoliths make excellent camera studies while the caves are the perfect answer to an age-old question: Where shall we put old razor-blades?

Back to Moncton, and out on Route 11 you are in the land of jawbreaking Indian names. Our old friends the Maliseets and Micmacs outdid themselves with such names as Buctouche, Richibucto, Kouchibouguacis, and Kouchibouguac. But what gives me quivering wonderment is who decided to keep those names? After all, when junior gives off sounds like that we wait until he can talk. I was more interested in how Upper Bay of Wine (Upper Baie du

Vin) got its name, but the first few natives gave me *"qui sait?"* So that's one investigation I'm leaving for you. It sounds promising. Chatham, near the mouth of the Miramichi, is the end of the paved road. However, Route 8 up to Bathurst isn't too risky.

Bathurst and Beyond

BATHURST IS as near perfect a place as any coming read-
ily to mind, to challenge those persons who say, with
conviction: "The New Brunswick salmon move in perpetual migration from the sea, to lay their eggs in the
stream where they were hatched years before, and in no
other." I'd like to see one of these people prove it. This
facetious aside disposed of, Bathurst has much for the ordinary tourist and for the sportsman. It is situated at the
head of a basin by its own name, on the Baie des Chaleurs,
which is French for "We-Swear-That-Water's-Warm," even
if it chills you.

Youghall Beach, six miles away, has been called "Canada's perfect sea beach" by experts, and who am I to dis-
pute them, even if I stubbed my toe on a log in the sand?
Nepisiguit Bay curls around Bathurst like Manolete
curved the fighting bulls around his body. The river by
the same name is rated by at least one sportsman's magazine as the best trout stream in North America. And there
are three other rivers near by. Guides have their headquarters at the headwaters of the Nepisiguit and Tetagouche.
And there is a famous canoe trip hereabouts, up the
Nepisiguit and down the Tobique, which takes three
days. Bathurst has a nine-hole golf course, and a few miles
up the bay is Kent Lodge, up to date. (Also Ingle-Neuk
Lodges, Kennock Van, Twilight Cabins, Carleton Hotel,
Gloucester Hotel and Salmon Beach Camps in town or
near by.) From Bathurst you may charter a plane to fly to

47

the hunting lodge of your dreams and a famous R.A.F. ace may be the pilot. Several of them own the Bathurst Air Services.

From here the drive around Gloucester County's peninsula (which, I take it, is the Miscou or Shippigan Peninsula) on Route 11, is rewarding, sort of a poor man's Gaspé Peninsula tour.

Up along the Warm Water Bay, Route 11 to Dalhousie and Campbellton, you travel through pretty, small-wooded country, seemingly always fragrant, and know that you didn't come to New Brunswick to spend your time in some of her cities. En route there are the Bonaventure Lodges at New Mills, lodges set in a park, with splendid view, al fresco dining, and everything reasonably priced and in harmony with the lovely countryside. Here on the Restigouche are the famous silver salmon, for which some sportsmen would sell a badly battered soul. There are car ferries to Quebec and there is a rejuvenating drive to Matapedia, which, if your visit is in the fall, when nature is doing a slow burn, is much recommended. There are the high Quebec hills in the distance and little worlds of their own in view, green islets in the river. Best place to stay in Campbellton: the Chateau Restigouche. In the area: Sanfar Camps, where filet mignon is a specialty.

At Matapedia I spent a week end in a dreary hotel just across from the railroad station, listening to the True Story of the Dungarvon Whooper. It was a long, wandering yarn about various camps being visited by a wild-eyed, tattered hermit who gave out with screams at night. This yo-yo and his successors have been operating in the more remote regions since 1870. Many a campfire sitter has been regaled with this serialized, sexless, fresh-air version of *Gone With the Wind*. The province's publicity mill recently ground out an eleven-page story on the Whooper, carefully pointing out he hasn't been heard from recently. As has been previously noted, Route 17 down to St. Leonard isn't first rate, so we'll skip over that lightly. We'll hop from St. Leonard up to Edmundston, so we can begin at the top of New Brunswick's star route, Number 2.

Edmundston, the northern gateway to New Brunswick, has a paper company which shoots pulp across the international bridge through a pipe, for the making of paper in Madawaska, Maine. It is another center for outfitting hunting parties and a good spot to hire a canoe for the St. John River excursion. (New Royal Hotel; Madawaska Inn; either, $3.50 to $5.00, American plan. On Route 2, Theriault's Tourist Home.)

Back through St. Leonard (which is across from Van Buren, Maine) and down Route 2 to Grand Falls, where we are back on Broadway, however improbable. Route 2 through the town was widened to deserve the name "Broadway." Grand Falls is the locale for a very pretty legend of sacrifice, which, chances are, is true. Our story opens with the capture of Malabeam, Maliseet maiden, by fierce, marauding Mohawks. They stuffed the fair maiden in their war canoe and twisted her arm to make her reveal where the home village was located. She told them a certain distance down the river but neglected to inform them about the wicked falls in between. So they, together with Malabeam, plunged to their deaths. But the village was saved. Thus the Indian name for the place, Chik-im-ik-pe, meaning "Destroying Giant." Grand Falls is a spectacle well worth seeing, even if you've seen Niagara. They've harnessed its 225-foot fall, and the largest water-pressure tunnel in Canada passes right under the center of town. There is a courteous reception waiting for you if you wish to tour the power plant.

Perth and Andover, seven miles from Fairfield, Maine,

are near the famous Tobique hunting and fishing area. This is in the general vicinity of Rocky Brook, which George Allen, famous New Brunswick guide, gives as the locale of one of his tallest bear stories: According to Allen he was "boiling his kettle," or cooking his food, when a big bear chased him up a tree. Spotting a hole in the trunk, Allen figured there'd be another one below where he could crawl out, so he popped in, just a split second ahead of the bear. He crawled down—and ran into another bear, plugging up the nether end. And now above him came the big irascible fellow. Trapped in a hollow tree between two bears! It sounded like a script for a Frank Morgan broadcast. But Allen knew the bear always backs down a tree. So he got out his hunting knife and jabbed that big fellow above, who now had his feet on Allen's head. As he stabbed the bear in the rumble seat Allen grabbed the beast's tail, and like jet propulsion (it says here in the prepared notes handed me) the bear zoomed out of there. Allen had the presence of mind to let go of the tail just as he saw the light, so that he and the bear parted company with a lot of tree between them.

There's an Indian reservation near by, and Indian guides available, so what happened to Allen needn't to you. York's Riverview Cabins, at Andover, are recommended, along with the restaurant, and Ann's at Perth.

The peaceful little town of Hartland has a claim to fame because of its having the longest covered bridge in the world, accounting for 1,282 feet of the province's estimated eight miles, total length, of covered bridges. Did you ever wonder why they put covers on bridges? Experts in New Brunswick tell us the answer is simple. The bridges last longer that way.

Woodstock is known as the central gateway to New Brunswick, for tourists coming in from Bangor and Houlton, Maine. Sportsmen stop here to buy and pack bacon and beans for the hunting and fishing territory near by. (If you stop in Woodstock, the Carlisle Hotel is recommended.)

Traveling in the shade and over pleasant, well-engineered bends in the "country" road, with interesting views of the river at every turn and glimpses of quiet, white churches, some with the lich gates where the dead are rested before final interment; through little villages where people have led unexciting but satisfying lives, we come to the capital, Fredericton.

As a city it is still saying "Twenty-three skiddoo," and let us hope it never gets hep to the jive. For as it is, it's unique and there should always be some place on earth with its qualities. I've never seen another capital with so much shade, or a daily newspaper which has been left so far in the shade. It is called the *Fredericton Gleaner,* and there are days when the editor and the reader glean little but pride and prejudice. Watch for the Four o'Clock Edition—it's the only one they've got! And read the editorials; you'll find them everywhere except in the want ads, editorials such as B. Franklin might have written. If they ever lose the mold, the rhythm or the all-around pattern for a "quaint" old English city, Fredericton will serve. (Best hotels: Windsor, Queen, and Barker; or, six miles west on Route 2, Holyoke Tourist Cottages, for angling at Hartt's Island Pool.) Fredericton has a cathedral which seems to have been lifted in one piece and whirled to the New World: Christchurch Cathedral, one of the most stately edifices on the American continent, and the first cathedral *foundation* established on British soil since the Norman Conquest in 1066.

The story of the cathedral's building was told me by Horace M. Block, assistant director of the provincial Bureau of Information and Tourist Travel, who acted as my host while I visited. Mr. Block, a journalism graduate of Columbia University, is a good reporter.

"It took eight years to build the cathedral," he told me. "Eight years of toil for workmen but a lifetime of effort for one or two others—and a bit of a mystery, besides. The pioneer Metropolitan Bishop of the Church of England in Canada, the Most Reverend John Medley, D.D., got the foundation laid in 1845. Soon afterward funds dried up on him, and after a fruitless meeting with the building committee, during which the others decided to enclose what had been built and let matters rest, the Bishop prayed all night. Next morning he received a gift of £500, about $2,500 in those days, from England in the mail. The gift bore only the initials 'F.S.M.' You may go there now and see 'F.S.M.' carved into one of the stones supporting the chancel near the Bishop's seat. No one knows to this day who 'F.S.M.' was. Well, the work went on, and during it a traveling salesman for a Bristol, England, tea house brewed some help for the Bishop. Each day after he had worked for his employer he repeated his rounds for the cathedral, and got subscriptions of another $2,500. And so it went, to completion. In 1896 they placed a cenotaph in the south transept, with recumbent effigy of Bishop Medley, but in a larger sense the building itself is his memorial."

We drove around looking at the construction of the new hotel which will bear the name of Lord Beaverbrook, born Max Aitken, who grew up at Newcastle, New Brunswick. We visited the University of New Brunswick, which permeates the city's intellectual life as few citadels of learning ever do. And we sat in Mr. Block's office quietly amused as Geraldine Kinney, secretary-receptionist, ruled all with the hand of a gentle dictator. Mr. Block and his associate,

Fred H. Phillips, talked about poets, of which Fredericton has had several; and the last fatal duel in New Brunswick. They told how the compound marine engine was invented in the capital, and said that near by there once was a man so headstrong he gave the world the phrase the "Main John." We also discussed the probability that the Fredericton frog, over in the Barker Hotel lobby, supposed to have weighed forty-two pounds, was a fraudulent croaker. But all we arrived at was: "Forty-two pounds is a lot of tadpole."

The duel took place back in 1821. After some inflaming words over the issuance of a writ, two lawyers subpoenaed each other to a pistoling on Maryland Hill, and one of them, George L. Wetmore, was killed, which seems a bit drastic; but I should think the pattern set more honest than present-day practice, where they get hot at each other and then both shoot their clients, financially.

"Benjamin Franklin Tibbitts invented the compound marine engine which would utilize steam under both high and low pressures," said Mr. Block. "Getting financial backing here in Fredericton was difficult, but eventually he built an engine and a boat, launching them in 1843. On the day his boat slid into the water the town's idle were on the shores, ready with ridicule. But it was successful, and they remained to cheer. In 1847 Tibbitts built a boat for regular commercial trips between Saint John and Grand Lake. Seven years later, Tibbitts, only forty, lay dying at his home on the shore of the lake. That night his ship, ablaze to the water's edge and abandoned by her crew, drifted down toward the Tibbitt home, and the man and his work became dust and ashes simultaneously. I often wonder whether Tibbitt, who gave the world something new, looked out and saw that fire."

Mr. Phillips told the story of the "Main John" Glasier. John, associated with his brother Stephen in lumbering, was such a hard bargainer contractors avoided him and dealt with Stephen. To which John protested: "I am the main man." Paddy McGarrigle, an Irish cook, heard that petulancy once too often and tabbed Glasier with the name the world now associates with any man too concerned with his own prerogatives. "Main John," by the way, started a one-man war with the state of Maine, but Maine just wouldn't fight. Construction of dams on tributaries of the St. John over in Maine having lowered the volume of water on the river, "Main John" went over and blew up the Allagash River dam below Churchill Lake, and got himself a rise of three feet of water at Grand Falls, 160 miles distant. If the Maine men had come over, "Main John" would have tried to take them all on at once, no doubt. It is safe to say there isn't anyone like "Main John" in Fredericton today.

Besides Lord Beaverbrook, who has recently bought a home in Fredericton and has been installed as Chancellor of the University, New Brunswick can boast of Andrew Bonar Law (born at Rexton, Kent County), the only Prime Minister of England born outside the British Isles, and Right Honorable Viscount Richard Bedford Bennett, Prime Minister of Canada from 1930 to 1935, who was born at Hopewell and reared at Chatham, New Brunswick. Sir Charles G. D. Roberts, Bliss Carman, and Francis Joseph Sherman, three of Canada's best bards, called Fredericton home. The residence of Bliss Carman may be visited, over on Shore Street. In some of the old wooden chairs you'll see over there he may have sat with his friend, Mark Twain, or as he composed some of his famous lines in *Pipes of Pan.*

Bliss Carman might almost have been thinking of you tourists when he wrote:

> And so you shall come without cunning
> But wise in the simple lore,
> To the house of the Little Brothers,
> And God will open the door.

· 5 ·

Last Outpost of Leisure and Dream

WHAT DID the Lieutenant Governor of Mississippi say to the Lieutenant Governor of Prince Edward Island? He said, "You have an air-cooled, windswept, sun-kissed, wave-washed country—the most beautiful I have ever seen." Either Jacques Cartier or John Cabot discovered it. Cartier described it as "the fairest land that it may be possible to see." Cabot said, "The land is excellent and the climate temperate." The earliest Micmacs called it "Minegoo," meaning *the* Island," which implied, as its present owners always do: What other island *IS* there? According to Micmac legend, the Island's bright red soil was colored Abegweit red, gayest of them all, by Glooscap, the Micmac and Maliseet demigod, because he sought a cheerful, cozy place to retire when the sameness of the mainland bored him. The Islanders today want to know, seriously, whether a demigod's special retreat is good enough for you. L. M. Montgomery, author of *Anne of Green Gables,* said the Island was "last outpost of leisure and dream."

The guidebooks call it "Canada's only island province," "Cradle of Confederation," or "Birthplace of Canada," and "Garden of the Gulf." As Lawrence J. Burpee wrote: "The true Islander is never completely happy away from his Island . . . and the rest of us are with him a hundred per cent in July and August!"

There are only three drawbacks: there aren't enough first-class hotels, first-class roads, or first-class tourist

months in the season over there. You have June, July,
August, and September—and eight little winters.

You may come to Prince Edward Island by automobile,
train, or bus (crossing over on one of two ferries), by transport or private plane, and by boat. It is simple by bus or
train. Just buy your ticket to Charlottetown and they'll get
you there. Driving your own car, take either of two ferries. If you are driving in New Brunswick (or any area
which makes that the logical approach) take Route 2
through Moncton and Sackville to Aulac, New Brunswick,
then change to Route 16 to Cape Tormentine. There, for
$3.00 (round trip) per car and 65 cents (round trip) for
passengers, you may drive aboard the luxurious *Abegweit,*
largest ferry of her type ever built, with good restaurants,
and more modern in some ways than the *Queen Mary.*
You land at Port Borden and take Route 2 to Charlottetown. Or, if coming from Nova Scotia, you will find the
other ferry closer. Starting from Cariboo (near Pictou) you
go to Wood Islands, Prince Edward Island, where you
must take a slightly less satisfactory road, Route 4, until
you come upon Route 3 to Charlottetown. Tickets on the
two ferries are interchangeable.

There are boats from Boston and Montreal and anchor-
ages for private yachts in all the main ports. The Island
has good airfields at Charlottetown and Summerside.

But since the province is so small (the Island is only 110
miles long, and from two to thirty miles wide) you would
do well, if motoring, to stay in either Charlottetown, the
capital (population 12,000), or Summerside. You may motor in a day to almost any point, and easily return. The
Charlottetown, a Canadian National hotel, is by far the
best place to stay, but you had better have reservations
far in advance. Last year the place was bulging at its plush
seams. (Rates from $6.26 single and $11.02 double, very

fine meals included.) Other hotels, the Queen, the Lennox, the Russ, and the Oakleigh (when they serve meals, they average $3.50 to $4.25 a day per person), are fair. There are a host of private homes renting rooms and serving meals (names can be secured by writing the Prince Edward Island Travel Bureau, 101 Queen Street, Charlottetown).

The main attraction in Charlottetown is the Province Building, where representatives of various provinces met to consider union of the British North American Colonies, September 1, 1864. The Confederation Chamber has been restored as it was when the historical events occurred, as very few such venerated chambers have been. As you stroll about inside the shiny handrails, examining respected gifts and relics, plaques and documents, you may understand why this high-ceilinged room is well-nigh sacred to Canadians. I got to visit it under slightly unusual circumstances. Because of a hectic schedule at this point in my travels (which made me realize how John Gunther must feel to visit fifteen countries in thirty days and write the definitive, inside story straight from the Trojan Horse's mouth) it was necessary to open the historical room for me on a Sunday. But this was done, cheerfully, by the temporary archivesman, James Carregher, of the Treasury Department. I was accompanied by A. A. Leaman, who as district passenger agent for the Canadian National Railways has set some sort of a record: he's still cheerful, shyishly humorous, and even feels friendly towards his ulcers. They must have mistaken me for one of those important writers on sex and history whose books sell into the millions, well Cerf-tified. Because they asked me to sign the Distinguished Guests register, not far from the signatures of Field Marshal Montgomery and Lord Alexander. It was a very pleasant and impressive morning, and just this once I'm glad there wasn't anyone around to point out that the action taken in this historic Chamber was the obvious thing, the predestined thing, motivated partially by fear that the United States would strike back for the overt acts committed by British North America while the American Confederacy was making its gallant but futile bid.

It was at Charlottetown that I first heard about the "thirsty plague." This is the forerunner of a bad case of galloping hangover. Once the symptom has been noted, you drop down to the doctor, canapés in one hand, and the conversation goes something like this:

PATIENT: I'm very thir—sick, doc, and need a prescription, bad.

DOCTOR: Just how sick are you?

PATIENT: About three quarts worth, er, pretty sick, doc.

DOCTOR: I know it's rather hard to tell, in advance, how long this sickness will last, but how often do you get these urges, or symptoms?

PATIENT: Just about every week end. Better fix me up for six months, doc.

DOCTOR: That'll be three dollars, please.

(Exit with a thirsty gleam.)

There are less than 90,000 people living on Prince Edward Island. Some of them, doubtless, are children, or Prohibitionists, or malfunctioners with bad livers. Yet the province had made $600,000 profit on liquor for the first eight months of 1947, my sources reported.

The capital is fairly impressive, for a city of 12,000, with comfortable-looking houses set back in pleasant lawns, well shaded. But the countryside is even nicer. Where Nova Scotia was wind, wood, and water, the Island is not too heavily wooded, with gently rolling, obviously fertile fields, healthy-looking cattle, and tiny boats riding in sheltered coves. Prince Edward Island seems for all the world like a Bermuda set miles out of place to the north. Here and there are fox farms, but the boom Charles Dalton started when he proved foxes could be kept and bred in captivity, 'way back in 1887, has largely subsided. There was something in the climate which brought their fur out just right, and there still is. But by now too many other persons and places are "in the act."

Perhaps the first logical trip out from Charlottetown should be to the Prince Edward Island National Park area, which extends as a coastline strip for nearly twenty-five miles along the north shore and includes some of the finest beaches in Eastern Canada—reddish in color and beaten smooth and broad by action of the surf. On these beaches can be seen some of Nature's finest works of art, and all the Venuses have arms—and suntanned thighs. Take Route 6 and turn left onto Route 16, to get to Dalvay House, where administrative headquarters of the park are located, and which also is a hotel for forty-five guests, first come, first served. You will be only about two hundred yards from the beach. Take a look at the map to see where the road takes you around the park area. The next place is Stanhope, which has a fine beach, but the hotel is not first class. Shaw's and Gregor's hotels at Brackley (accommodation, combined, for 125) are fair, but toilet facilities are half a sleeper-jump down the hall. Cavendish, where we find *Anne of Green Gables* country everywhere we look (the house, the Lover's Lane, Haunted Wood, and so on) has a golf course, a bathhouse near the beach, and a campground—everything, in fact, but the commodious hotel which the place demands. In the United States the problem would be one of zoning; here it is one of getting someone to make an investment in a sure thing. Meanwhile, the Links Inn, at Cavendish, is good, but only for the first twenty people who come along. (And bathing is a mile away.)

Near here is the small but interesting town of Rustico, where in 1866, and thus many years before Henry Ford schemed up his first Model T (for transportation, economical), Father Belcourt showed nine hundred guests his automobile. "A steam carriage was put in motion," read an account in the *Charlottetown Examiner* a week later, "and with great wonder and delight was observed steaming away for half a mile on the road and back again, at a fast rate of speed."

"With great wonder and delight" you, too, may "steam" down to the south shore, to Keppoch, only about five miles from Charlottetown, where the Dunbar House and Cottages and Bayfield House are located—and recommended. Bathing is good here at high tide.

From Charlottetown you may get to Summerside by train or by driving down Route 20. Summerside is another good harbor, another good, thriving town. The best places to stay there: Queen Hotel, Mulberry Lodge, Bonnie Brae Inn, Garden of the Gulf Cabins, and Harbour View Cabins and Cottages. (Reasonable in every instance. Example: $3.71 per day per person at Queen Hotel, including meals.) Many of the Summerside restaurants serve the famous Malpeque oysters in season; they are found in the bay of the same name, near by. You may drive your car, on Route 1, all the way to Tignish if you wish, and the trip in fair weather will whisk you back to scenes of your childhood, no matter where that really occurred; the Island has that quality.

If you want to know where that vulgar bit of comeback, "Oh, yeah," originated, drive to the eastern terminus of Route 3, the Brudenelle Point district, where once lived an ill-starred genius named Jean-Pierre de Roma. Monsieur de Roma's biography gives the double-strength, reverse-action "huzzah" to the writers of those corny copy-

book maxims: "When at first, etc.," and "Success is the
result of steady application," or write your own static.
For here De Roma began to build himself an empire. The
first bug in his balm came when his partners quit, cold.
Our hero bought them out and continued. Some New
Dealers of those days (this was 1732) talked his settlers
into leaving him. He got more. They raised big crops.
Came mice in such droves the plagues of Egypt were a
comparative inconvenience. De Roma merely sat himself
down and wrote a treatise on the mice who were eating
the grass and every living thing except the humans and the
mules. And he kept his people alive by farming the sea.
Next his largest ship, with all its cargo, was lost in transit.
Four years later, by hard labor, he had recouped his losses
and was once more confident of his colony's future. So, out
of the tall timbers stomped a goon-band of New England-
ers, who in a few minutes wiped out the fruits of thirteen
years of hard toil. De Roma and his family escaped into
the forests and got to Quebec the hard way. He continued
working eighteen hours a day until his death, but just
couldn't get ahead. There isn't any moral. Just file the
De Roma story away as an antidote to the inevitable
spouter of sweetness and light, professional Rotarian, slo-
ganeer, or believer in the Horatio Alger–Ben Franklin–
Saturday Evening Post formula; there's one in every party.

Also from Charlottetown, Route 6 is a comfortable drive
to Tracadie, former home of Sir William MacDonald, who
never smoked but made a fortune out of advertising the
weed and selling it to others; to Souris, which has seen
three visitations of mice, but none since 1738, and thence
as far east as the railroad goes, to Elmira or Lakeville (on
Route 6) but not to East Point, out on the rim, because the
road is doubtful. After that you may double back on 6A

along the battering Gulf of St. Lawrence, excellent for views. Out there at East Point, the spot was well named by our old friends, the Micmacs: They called it "Kespemene-gek," or literally, "End of an Island." To us it is the end of *The Island*. And we're off to do Quebec.

· 6 ·

Le Canada Français

SOME DEMON statistician has figured out that there is room in the province of Quebec for all the people in the world to sit down—and for the British among them to keep their proper distance until introduced. At any rate, the province is the largest in Canada, with an area exceeding the combined areas of England, France, the three Maritime Provinces, New York State, all of New England, and the State of California. From east to west it stretches 1,350 miles, which is nearly half the distance across the United States from New York to California, and it runs northward to Baffin Land. Even that part which is water is considerably larger than England. Nearly two-thirds of it is unexplored.

It includes Montreal, Canada's largest city; Quebec, this hemisphere's only walled city north of Mexico, and the place which gives the average American the biggest bang out of a trip to Canada; and it embraces the great St. Lawrence waterway, which is the heart of America and can not be matched anywhere on earth. It has perfect ski slides and ski weather, along with good transportation facilities, so that people from the great population centers of the United States may acquire that hard-sought winter tan, that exhilarating winter rejuvenation. The place has everything but the Rockies, and it has the heights next biggest rising sheer out of the middle of a lake, so help me.

Listen to this, from an official bulletin:

"We, all of us, of *La Province de Quebec* invite you

most warmly to come and see us, confident that you will be *enchanté* with the comfort, the relaxation, the sheer happiness that come from the traditional welcome of *le Canada français*. We are just across a frontier, wide open and hospitable. But once you cross into *La Province,* you will be transported to old Normandy and old Brittany. Some have called us 'France in America.' We are more than that; we are *Old France.* For more than three hundred years, we have been rooted in this Quebec soil we love so much. Many of us, even today, live on the very piece of land cleared by the 'first ancestor' who came over to *La Nouvelle France* when the kings of France held court at Versailles. And, in all that we believe precious, we have retained the traditions of our forefathers.

"In our home and family life, in our way of doing a million things we remain devotees of the gracious life, or, as we say, *la vie gracieuse.* You will find a tempo of living less hurried; geared to allow more time for enjoying the beauties with which our land is endowed.

"So come and see us in *La Province.* Enjoy our wine-like atmosphere, our sunshine, our sea and mountains, our lakes and dales. Revel in our hunting and fishing, our skiing and tobogganing. Drive down our fine highways, through *coquet* villages with peaked roofs and shining church spires. Bow at our shrines, visit our historic monuments. Compare the peace of venerable towns with the bustle of our great cities and ports. Taste—and relish—our *cuisine-française.* Revel with us in the glories which deft fingers produce—cunning works in wool and flax, metal and pottery. We are sure that, altogether, you will enjoy your French-Canadian vacation.

"*La Province de Quebec* says: '*Bienvenue!*' "

The manner in which Americans respond to this type of invitation may be gauged by the fact that 15,000,000

persons are unofficially estimated to have visited Quebec
Province last year. The whole of Canada has only slightly
over 11,000,000 population.

Why go to Quebec? There is, of course, a different answer for winter and for summer. In winter, the chances are
you'd be going skiing, up in the Laurentians just beyond
Montreal, in the Lac Beauport region near the city of
Quebec, or on some gentle slope of your own, or your
party's choosing in the Eastern Townships. Or you could
be coming to participate in that increasingly popular game
of curling, which is somewhat like shuffleboard on ice; or
just going to Montreal at any time because, like myself,
you believe it one of the most delightful cities on earth:
like Paris, only better, with the gingerbread and the yell-
ing, demonstrating mobs deleted. In the summertime, of
course, you might want to go to any one of the thousands
of watering places where cool breezes blow; to the Eastern
Townships, to the wonderful city of Quebec, which stands
for exactly what it stood for when it was founded, 340
years ago; or to the Gaspé Peninsula: ancient, rural France
along a picturesque shore. These things, plus hunting,
fishing, rubbernecking, and cool cruises on the incomparable Saguenay and the majestic St. Lawrence. Or, in case
you're a prospector, the gold mines of Abitibi, north of
the Laurentians.

In Quebec, all roads lead to Montreal. And for the citi-
zens of the States going into Quebec most roads do, too.
From New York, via Malone, take U.S. 10 and P.Q. 4 to
Montreal; by way of Rouse's Point, Highways 9 and 9A to
Montreal; from Vermont, by way of Swanton, Highway 7
to Montreal; via Newport and Rock Island, Highway 5 to
Sherbrooke and then Route 1 to Montreal or Quebec City.
(Via Stanhope, Route 22 to Sherbrooke.) From New
Hampshire, through Comin's Mills, take Route 27 to

Sherbrooke; from Maine, by way of Jackman, Route 23 to Levis and Quebec. (Via Megantic, Route 34 to Trois-Rivières and 24 to Saint-Georges, then 23 to Levis and Quebec.) From Ontario, by way of Cornwall, take Route 2 to Montreal; via Ottawa, Routes 8, 17, and 29 to Montreal.

From New Brunswick, by way of Edmundston, follow Route 2 to Rivière du Loup. The Delaware and Hudson, Boston and Maine, Rutland, and Central Vermont, among other United States railroads, link with the Canadian National Railways, the Canadian Pacific Railway, and the Quebec Central into the province. Airlines: Colonial, from Washington and New York; Northeastern, from Boston; Trans-Canada from Chicago, Detroit, Cleveland and other points west, as well as from the Maritime provinces, bring you into Montreal. Inside the province the Canadian Pacific Air Lines serve Montreal, Quebec, Chicoutimi, Mont Joli, Rimouski, and Baie-Comeau. Or, if you're the type that has a yacht left, come down the Great Lakes, the Lachine Rapids, and the St. Lawrence to Montreal, thence along the St. Lawrence or Saguenay. Still another favored course is out of Lake Champlain, through the Richelieu River to the St. Lawrence. And here's hoping you can coax the sun down over the yardarm early in the day, just like the British Navy!

It was Joe H. Fountain, New York representative of the Canadian National Railways, who really made me acquainted with Montreal. Fountain, a somewhat smaller, Vermont version of the actor, William Powell, belies his family name. His manner of being helpful was to see that I got around and talked to the people. With his dry, shy manner he could get more attention from Montreal citizens than Lana Turner could from a boatload of sailors just back from an unbroken six months' cruise.

From previous visits I already knew the quick and easy

facts about Canada's metropolis. That it was the second largest French-speaking city on earth, and the greatest inland port, with ocean liners tied up more than eight hundred miles from the ocean. That it was located on an island formed by the St. Lawrence and the Ottawa rivers. That its million to million and a half people represent more than one-tenth of Canada's population, and during a year play host to many more millions. And that all this curious mixture of skyscrapers, shrines, slums, tony hotels, and sleazy dives can be seen from the top of Mount Royal, balcony to one of the world's truly grown-up municipalities.

We visited the Place d'Armes, historical heart of the city, where sleepy French soldiers grumbled at reveille on frosty mornings three hundred years ago. What impressed me there was the irony of the fact that the statue of Paul de Chomedey de Maisonneuve, founder of Ville-Marie (which became gay and quixotic Montreal), is right next to the Bank of Montreal. For De Maisonneuve was a mystic who cared nothing for worldly goods but sought to convert the Indians, even if his doing so was going to result in all their deaths. In this very plaza, De Maisonneuve fought the savage Iroquois. From here left seventeen youths to block the path of seven hundred attacking braves at the Long Sault. They died in a wilderness Verdun in miniature, after fighting for eight days, smashing the fierce invaders and saving the city.

From the house not far away went La Salle on his expeditions, and Pierre le Moyne d'Iberville, founder of Louisiana, and his brother, De Bienville, founder of New Orleans. And, too, Jacques Porlier, founder of Green Bay, Wisconsin, and Salomon Juneau, founder and first mayor of Milwaukee, started out from ancient Montreal.

On the rim of the Place d'Armes is Notre Dame, Parish

Church of Montreal, built in 1824 on the site of a church erected 150 years before that, and containing the largest bell in North America, aptly called *"Le Gros Bourdon,"* which weighs twelve and one-half tons. There is a legend that canny French-Canadians can detect the accent of anyone reared within the sound of this bell. The Sulpician Seminary, built in 1683, is next to the church, and there is a huge inner garden which has been a cloister for men's thoughts for 265 years, no matter what is going on outside. Through the good offices of Claude Melançon, Canadian National Railways' representative on the French-Canadian radio "brains trust," or sort of *Information, Please,* we were able to see and understand it.

Perhaps the oldest and quaintest church in Montreal is the Church of the Bonsecour, known as "the sailors' church."

"It has been written," said Mr. Melançon, "and I can only quote: 'The French-Canadian is at peace with this world and the next.' "

With a short, brisk walk we were in the city-hall area, with the statue to Lord Nelson at the head of busy, pleasantly odorous and colorful Bonsecours Market. We watched a fat matron being helped from her limousine by a liveried chauffeur, after which she waddled here and there by grunt-propulsion, pinching the vegetables. Spread out before her and the charwomen and ordinary housewives with whom she vied were the perishable harvests of a prodigious province: everything from a gooseberry to a goose. And flowers. But no wine. That is one important way in which it differed from a French market: no wine. And there were no secondhand book or magazine kiosks.

Next we came to the building which is probably first in appeal to Americans taking a pony of history, neat. It is the Chateau de Ramezay, built in 1705, home of the early governors of Montreal, scene of many a famous flirtation and long-forgotten love. Here the invading troops of the American Revolutionary army had headquarters in 1775. Here Benedict Arnold, that great soldier, first sulked in prideful introspection, and here Benjamin Franklin came, too, as the first Propaganda Warfare Department of an American army, trying to parlay his wit, wisdom, and a hatful of type into a French-Canadian uprising against the British at the side of the American revolutionists. It was in this very building that the good doctor realized he had failed, packed fifty-four personal articles (including a deck of cards and a pair of socks), and went home in time to sign the Declaration of Independence. (How much more full of the joy of life was Franklin than those who have adopted him today and parrot his pious public utterances, but never his ribaldry!) But a French printer he left behind started the *Montreal Gazette,* which is still functioning.

In the Chateau, itself a perfect museum piece of rounded towers and sentry shelters, the Numismatic Society of Montreal has set up a museum of Canadiana. I looked in vain for the garter of the girl who almost kept Lord Nelson in Canada and thus might have changed the course of history.

We traipsed around the east end of the city, with its excellent view of the harbor and its triple iron stairways leading like ornate individual fire escapes into the front of the homes. Made to order for young folks at the mating period of life, I am reliably informed they were built to obviate the waste of inner hallways.

With George Herbert Lash, assistant director of Canadian National Railways' public relations, the perfect companion, perfect Canadian, and perfect host, we lunched and dined at such places as Café Martin, Drury's English Inn,

Quebec is the only walled city on the continent north of Mexico. Old Saint Louis Gate through which the victorious British troops marched after they defeated Montcalm's army and ended French rule of Canada.

Ste. Anne de Beaupré, shrine in Quebec City, where many thousands of faithful believe cures occur through miracles.

At the tip of the Gaspé Peninsula, Bonaventure Island's cliffs and beaches offer unequaled refuges for cormorants, gannets, and gulls.

A bit of the Gaspé Peninsula. Offshore is the famous pierced rock from which near-by village of Perce, tourist mecca, gets its name.

Largest city in Canada, Montreal is 85 per cent French speaking and has as distinctive a flavor as any city on the American continent. Ocean-going ships ply the St. Lawrence River, shown in background.

St. Joseph's Oratory, Brother André's famed shrine, where countless visitors come seeking cures through miracles.

Winter near Morin Heights in Laurentian Mountains north of Montreal.

In winter, vacationists invade eastern Canada in force. Skiers hit the trail in the Laurentian Mountains, an ideal winter playground.

Along the St. Lawrence River at Sacre Coeur near Rimouski, Quebec.

Memorial in Ottawa commemorates heroic men and women of World War I.

Ontario's capital, Toronto, is second largest city in Canada and the most American in character of major cities of the eastern provinces.

Two hundred years ago *voyageurs* and trappers went into the bush much as do today's vacationists in Algonquin Park in northeastern Ontario.

Both Photos, Courtesy Canadian
National Railways

A Legislative building in
Regina. Body of water in
foreground is artificial
lake made from a swamp.

All that remains of original Fort Garry in Winni-
peg, metropolis of West.

the Windsor Steak House, Laurier's, Au Lutin Qui Bouffe, Aux Delices, and Chez Ernest's. (But there are scores of other pleasing restaurants in Montreal; the food is good and comparatively cheap, as a whole.)

There was much to see: The new ten-million-dollar station of the Canadian National Railways, St. James' Cathedral, which is a copy, at one-third the size, of St. Peter's in Rome, and therefore both impressive and of sentimental interest to those of the faithful who have been in Vatican City, or who know they can never go; McGill University campus, the former site of the Indian village, Hochelaga, which 413 years ago contained fifty large houses, "each lodging several families," according to Jacques Cartier, so you can see the housing situation is nothing new, only in those days a guy could scalp his mother-in-law if she washed her nylons in the spring.

But the highlight of the present visit was that sunny afternoon when Joe Fountain and his studious and likable co-worker, John Noel, took me by taxi and observation streetcar up the winding road to the top of Mount Royal. Cars aren't allowed inside the park, so we walked the last half mile or so along the roadway, being passed by couples and small families in horse-drawn cabs, or by equestrians on the bridle paths. Once on the Lookout, seven hundred feet above the city, we could see how the business monoliths had come like an irresistible flood from the water's edge to push the residences up on the mountain side. Up here you can tell Montreal has an architecture which is distinctive and good; that the thin church spires (there are 360 churches) and the 120 or so streets named after saints have been the giveaway: the Catholic Church is behind the plan and the venerability of Montreal's architecture. Up here there is an electrically lighted cross so many feet high that it can be seen for miles. It typifies the deep religious convictions of the people of Montreal. In a way, it *explains* Montreal.

In the Chateau near the Lookout historical murals depict the city's history. From the rim outside one may see the Green Mountains of Vermont and the Adirondacks in New York, while on extra-special days they say you may even "catch" the White Mountains back in New Hampshire.

"There are those who say," said Joe Fountain, looking down upon the city, "that Montreal is dirty, a tart whose lipstick is like her morals, too loud and not quite straight. But I say she has a soul and a future and that both may be detected here. After all, every city has slums. They're the dirty dishes in the sink of crowded civilization, everywhere. Why blame Montreal?"

Why, indeed?

On our way out we stopped to watch a photographer working with a pretty professional model on a horse, both of them ignoring a child model also hired for the afternoon, who was getting in a bit of mud-pie building. And we fed the ducks on the lake and later walked down to Remembrance Road, truly a fine name for a thoroughfare flanking a cemetery, and the streetcar.

But first we paused and gave thought to the faith which has transformed the face of the mountain through Brother André's famous St. Joseph's Oratory. Believers, some of them from thousands of miles away, were going up the four stages of sixteen steps on their knees, toward the huge pile of the Oratory where many scores of trusses, crutches, canes, and special paraphernalia for cripples testified, more eloquently than the written words framed and tossed there, to the help hundreds of persons had received from Brother André and to the faith he inspired.

"We can't all have the same ideas about this," said

Johnny Noel. "But whatever we think, it seems to me there just has to be a magnificent force here. For each one of these cases was a miracle, of course, right in the middle of our scientific times. Call it by the crassest name you can conjure, and it's still wonderful." And he did the research to show that Brother André, a runt of a man, a failure at everything for years, maligned by doctors who carped at his "cures" (which he never claimed, himself), accused of being an eccentric by his jealous contemporaries, was nevertheless a man of good humor, the very gay possessor of a sharp wit. He never took himself seriously. He attributed everything which transpired to faith and prayer. A woman complained to him that she had a weight on her chest. Brother André noted her décolleté dress and replied: "Well, it isn't the collar of your dress that bothers you. Pray until the cloth grows."

A little waitress-hostess in a midnight-snack restaurant summed things up for us, about Montreal and *La Province*. "What is it made Paris? Why, French women, monuments and park commissioners like your American Robert Moses, that's what! The Frenchman is close to the soil or he is close to the women, as clothes stylist, hairdresser, *parfumeur,* hotelkeeper, entertainer. Therefore the French-Canadian here in Montreal is either a hick, or altogether too slick, with pomaded hair and the suit with the zoot.

"But when Montreal becomes a state of mind, as Paris is, with a tradition to live up to, then she will get her Champs Elysées, and suddenly everyone will recognize the truth: that her women are ravishing and vital. The other nationalities in Quebec recognize that fact right now. In the large French families there are many girls, and there are always a few left over, after their sisters marry the French boys, to marry the Englishmen, Poles, and Scotsmen. Now here is where the church steps in, and this is what is happening to Canada; why it will someday be 'French.' . . . These French girls are brought up in the church, which means they will not practice birth control, and that there will be many babies, which will all belong to the church. They will be with Mamma, who is 'French' and they will be with the Mother Church. These people are more French than the French themselves. They were abandoned twice by France, once when they tried to fight against the English, and again when France had the revolution.

"France's high-born soldiers, adventurers, and cavaliers went back to France after Wolfe defeated Montcalm, there to die of gout or have their heads chopped off by revolutionists. The 60,000 people they left here have become eight to ten million. More than three and a half million are still in Canada, two million are in the United States, and the remainder are in Haiti, Martinique, and Central and South America. Montreal is three-fourths French, and all Canada is almost one-third. Because the British were in trouble with the American uprising they granted the Quebec Act, which allowed the French their language, their civil law, and their Church. Today they are the most powerful minority on earth, have a great 'say' in the British Commonwealth of Nations, and are on their way to a majority in Canada, the second greatest nation in the Commonwealth; they seek a national emblem and severance of ties from both England and France, and in their secret hearts even resent the alliance between the two European nations.

"Montreal already has more tourists and trade than Paris; Americans and Canadians, the only people with money to travel, can get to it without getting seasick. So one of these fine days it is destined to become the interna-

tional city for fun. Tired businessmen of the world will
come here to see chorus girls with rhinestones in their
navels.

"Me, gentlemen? My parents came from Devonshire."

"You have just heard the facts from one of the so-called
'little people,' " said Joe when we had regained the side-
walk. "Wonder why the French are so damned fecund here
and not in Europe? I can remember when the French 75
was an artillery piece, and now apparently, it's a family."

You who are seeking hotel rooms are the underdogs in
Montreal. I was treated very nicely at the Windsor, one of
the better hotels (with the Mount Royal), but the only
reason you need to know the names of Montreal hotels is
so you can write or wire for reservations. Some of them:
Berkeley, Ritz-Carlton, Queen's.

Several things about the Eastern Townships require re-
cording in our journal. They are considered the most
densely populated area of Canada (with forty-nine persons
to the square mile) and among the richest, with much
dairying and manufacturing. There are large and fertile
plains, rolling and semimountainous acres, and many
lakes and silvery watercourses. At Bolton East, near
Magog, Orford Mountain does a jack-in-the-box out of the
lake, 2,800 feet above sea level, the highest point in Canada east of the Rockies. Around the towns of Thetford
Mines, Asbestos, and Blake Lake are found the world's
richest deposits of asbestos; mines there produce two-thirds
of the world's supply of the mineral. There's also gold in
them thar foothills. Take Route 1 from either Montreal
or Valley Junction or intermediate points. In Sherbrooke,
the New Sherbrooke Hotel; Disraeli, the Hotel Disraeli;
Thetford Mines, the Hotel Commercial. Visiting my uncle, O. L. Dugan, at Newport Center, Vermont, my mother
used to recommend driving through Newport, taking

Route 5 to Sherbrooke, and Route 1 to Montreal. Route 7 from Swanton also leads you to a network of decent roads. From Route 9 you may also pick your route on first-class roads. This area will undoubtedly develop more in the near future, as far as tourists are concerned, because of the incontrovertible merits of Lakes Memphremagog (thirty miles long, largest in the district), Little Magog, Megantic, Brompton, Brome, and Aylmer.

The trip from Montreal to Quebec City, 164 miles which many a "quickie" traveler allots four hours to, can be interesting. True, there isn't much to detain you in the way of natural wonders. But the entire way through Quebec's heartland is history itself. This area, which you will traverse by way of Route 2 (Route 3 not being quite so good, but I suggest going one way and coming back the other) represented most of what was fair in the eyes of the favorites of the French Sun King. He granted them huge land areas, called seigniories. Men of proud regiments, national heroes, men of good, strong blood who had pushed the flag of France to the corners of the known earth, claiming spaces logistically impossible to maintain, were given rich lands, along with the bums of noble blood who happened to be sharing an unconsecrated couch with those women who occasionally slept with the king. The priests, too, and some of the various holy orders were given grants. And today you may stop and see some of their works and ruins.

Some of these farms you'll drive by and through have been in the same families for three hundred years. If you can speak a bit of French I'd suggest you stop in one or two of the general stores to buy some staple of traveling, such as tooth paste, or Kleenex, and talk to the people—farmers, nuns, traveling salesmen, fishermen. You've never seen anything like these stores, even though you're familiar with our all-embracing drug emporiums. For they have dresses, suits, sweaters, shoes, drugs, water closets, bathtubs, and some of them even take orders for heavy farm implements. Yet everything is compressed into a small space. I'd suggest you eat in one of the larger towns if you are not an experienced and enthusiastic traveler.

You are on the north bank of the St. Lawrence. The towns reflect their agricultural background, in the main, but here and there a small industry smokes up the air. Repentigny has a good beach, but the summer cottages are privately owned. At Saint-Sulpice, the ancient church has exquisite wood carvings. Berthierville, town of small industries, also boasts regular ferry service to the south shore, at Sorel.

Seals used to come up the St. Lawrence as far as Louiseville, which gave the town its first name, Saint-Antoine-de-la-Loup, seals being called *loups-marins,* or sea wolves, to differentiate them from the drugstore wolves, no doubt. Benjamin Gervais, father of the Minnesota municipality which bears his name, was born here. Yamachiche, next, is the Indian, or hard way to say River-Full-of-Clay, and the church here which reminds you of your childhood story books is copied after Roman basilicas.

Trois-Rivières, or Three Rivers, is about halfway to Quebec. It was founded 'way back in 1634, or eight years before they got around to putting a cross up at Mount Royal, Montreal, which you may be sure was the first thing they did. La Verendrye, said to have been the first white man to look upon the Rocky Mountains and what is now the state of Wyoming, was born here.

Here General Richard Montgomery stopped to rest, on his way to try to capture Quebec. The Recollet Monastery, built in 1699 and used as headquarters for British troops when they took over Canada, the elm-shaded Esplanade,

sort of a promenade built above the river on the walls of
old fortifications, and several ancient buildings impart a
unique atmosphere to the town. The town is the "downtown office" of a great and sprawling newsprint business
and the reception center for tourists coming to the St.
Maurice Valley for fishing, hunting, canoeing, motorboat-
ing, golf and tennis or winter sports. (In Trois-Rivières:
Hotel Chateau-de-Blois.)

At Cap-de-la-Madeleine the natives claim over 200,000
of the faithful annually make a pilgrimage to Notre-Dame-
du-Très-Sainte-Rosaire. Again, there are many venerable
buildings in Sainte-Anne-de-la-Perade. Grondines, which is
next, was named by Champlain, but no one ever thought
to ask the old gentleman why, and today nobody knows
what the name stands for or whence it came. At Descham-
bault you may see an old Hudson's Bay Company Post.
Portneuf is industrial, but Cap Santé has a reputation as a
country resort, a place where it is pleasant to lose yourself
for the summer. Donnacona is named, of course, after the
Indian chief Cartier took back to Europe from his first
voyage marked "Exhibit 'A' for Aborigine," to answer the
skeptics who didn't believe there were such things. The
next town is Les Ecureuils, which means "The Squirrels,"
and you can supply your own wisecracks. Newville is the
kind of a country resort I like, with a fine bathing beach.
Its church has paintings by Antoine Plamondon, who will
be recalled as a contemporary of Legaré.

If you believe you would rather stay outside Quebec
City, there are several recommended places in this area.
Near Sainte-Foy, which got its name from the road of the
same name on which Chevalier de Levis defeated the Brit-
ish General Murray in a bid to recapture Quebec (the Brit-
ish Navy came to the rescue of the garrison), there are Le
Domaine, Au Tour du Puits, and L'Auberge des Quatre-
Chemins.

· 7 ·

The Perfect Tourist Attraction

Aₙᴅ so we come to the almost perfect tourist attraction: Quebec City. It is almost totally French-speaking and the past is almost perfectly preserved there. To me, the essence of Quebec is that it was built a picture-book city. World-shaking events have taken place there, one of history's most decisive battles, for example, and yet the picture-book qualities remain, so that its walls and towers and stone battlements are a part of the living architecture; they are the tooth in which modern works have encroached only as a filling to replace decay.

It is as if an entire city were declared so full of memories that it must all be set aside as a historical park, and yet the people were allowed to go on living on the grounds; to go on driving automobiles over the cobblestones which have been drenched with the blood of heroes. Take the technicolor frames of the swashbuckling best of French period movies, history à la Hollywood; take the color series *Life* magazine did on the Middle Ages, bring them to life, and Quebec will match them. You can stroll about Quebec, making a score of new discoveries each day. Oh, I have visited older cities, much older. But they have had their faces lifted. They show the incisions and amputations of time. But the motto on the seal of Quebec Province is *"Je souviens,"* "I remember." And while there are those who believe that motto slightly sinister, I believe it refers to the French-Canadian desire to live with the past, as in his beloved Quebec City, ancient capital of French Canada.

To move from the dregs of the Lower Town to the pin-

nacle of Upper Quebec, the Chateau Frontenac and surrounding area, is ranging the social scale. Down below,
where on this earth the little people always seem to be,
there are narrow streets hedged by tall, dark, and ancient
buildings, with little garrets, smoke pots and dormer windows, exact replicas, at the time they were built, of the
tuberculosis incubators for the poor in Paris and Mar-
seilles. The people in them, for the most part, are Dick-
ensian characters with French accents, and their crutch
not gin but cognac and *vin*. The builders of these houses
had ample space, but they preferred to re-create an environ-
ment they knew, with the usual sound effects of women
screaming from one open window to the other. But, what
seems more incredible, they continued these duplex dun-
geons right up the side of the hill, using brick and stone
for stilts. You should see American tourists rattling around
these narrow, twisting streets and hear the young boys imi-
tating "Sharl Boy-ay," with "Come with me to zee Cas-
bah!"

On the way up the hill there are interesting restaurants
and grog shops. Driving a car up there, always in the
shadow of the rock, is adventure, because these steeply
slanted streets weren't built for the gasoline engine. Once
on top, say at the Chateau Frontenac, you are within walking distance of many things you will wish to see. And over
on Cape Diamond, like a gray skullcap on a fat and solemn
monk, lies the Citadel.

In the inner courtyard of Chateau Frontenac, which you
reach through a narrow gate in the towered, castle-like
stone chateau, I met Maurice Hebert, warmhearted ambassador of the Provincial Publicity Bureau, intelligent, pro-
fessorial, and interested. While waiting for Mr. Hebert I
met half a dozen American friends in the lobby of the
Chateau, a minor crossroads of the world, the Waldorf-

Astoria of the north, with medieval pinnacles, buttresses, and other trappings. Before striking out we located salient landmarks from the famous wooden esplanade, Dufferin's Terrace, not to be confused with Duffy's Tavern. On the site of the hotel, or slightly below it, Champlain built his original habitation. Now over the ruins is this town walk, lovers' lane, all-weather Easter Parade and Rubberneckers' Terrace. The young girls, like American newspapers, circulate and advertise; the men ogle and talk; married couples walk, talk, look at others, gossip, and see the sights. Down there below was the Lower Town, the wharfs, the water line which has wet many a hull identified in history, many a war canoe and boxlike man-of-war with her decks punctuated with smoothbore cannon and rough, rum-soaked, dissatisfied English or French seamen. It isn't hard to imagine what a stir the arrival of a man-of-war caused in the city, its flag determining whether it be greeted by bugles and guns or an opening wide of the city gates.

Down there, too, is the Isle of Orleans which, with the high bluffs, is responsible for the name "Quebec," "Where the Waters Narrow." Life down there is Normandy of four hundred years ago, except for the Canadian equivalent of the Sears-Roebuck catalog. And here is where bold Frontenac walked out his tense moments like Captain Hornblower on his quarterdeck, this gallant who could fight, write, bluff, cajole; who was at home talking to a duchess in her perfumed boudoir or a disaffected, savage sachem in his one-room utility tepee. As Bruce Hutchison has incomparably put it: "The appreciative modern world has conferred its highest honor on Frontenac. A cigar has been named after him."

The old Place d'Armes was roughly in the space in front of the Chateau Frontenac. On one end of Dufferin's Terrace is the Champlain monument. On the other end are the steps leading to the Citadel. We drove our car into the Citadel, but we would not have been able to had not Mr. Hebert been along. He pointed out a tiny brass cannon which the British brought away from Bunker Hill and left here for the Canadians to protect, where Americans can see it. It would not be hard to predict that some American athlete would carry it away for a watch fob, one foggy day. Near by are the buildings where F.D.R., Winston Churchill, Mr. King of Canada, and other prominent men met in their Quebec conferences. The Citadel is well preserved, with its parade grounds, dried-up moats, gun emplacements, and darkened runways to firing slits; even the night jar which was under the King of England's bed during his stay in 1939 is still there. From the walls we could look over the Plains of Abraham and the other fields where the battles have been fought, except General Montgomery's, since the Citadel wasn't built until after the English had won the city.

We drove around the Plains of Abraham, carefully noting each marker, and then down to the spot on the cliff where Wolfe came up from the beachhead, and won the country with one Commando raid. And we drove to Ste. Anne de Beaupré, another important shrine, where many thousands of people believe miraculous cures occur. Later, we paid a visit to Montmorency Falls, not far away. There, a few miles from the city (by automobile, Route 15, or the Quebec Railway runs out there), the Montmorency River is hosed 274 feet straight down—a hundred feet more of a drop than Niagara's! The big hotel near by is the former home of the Duke of Kent and his mistress.

Mr. Hebert and I lunched very pleasantly at Lac Beauport, both a summer and ski playground, about twenty minutes' drive from Quebec. From both the cocktail room and the restaurant there is a fine view of the lake, a shining cup set in a bowl of green. The food was excellent. There is a small hotel, with comfortable rooms, and native handicrafts are on sale in the lobby.

Back in the city we visited the carefully hidden spot where General Montgomery died while leading a charge of Americans through a snowstorm against the Quebec garrison on the last day of 1775. I'm not going to tell you where this spot is because I hope you will ask the Provincial Tourist people why it isn't in any of their historic tours, or in the printed material, or why it isn't better marked, at the same time that you ask, "Where the hell is it?"

Montgomery, whose brother helped Wolfe win Quebec, and who had often enjoyed a few drinks with Guy Carleton, who was defending Quebec, very badly needed a public-address system and Benjamin Franklin that night. Had he had them he might have won over the piddling number of soldiers who faced him. When Montgomery fell, dying, that ended the show. But had he won, who knows how history might have been changed? I wonder why the United States Government has not asked permission to put up a small monument commemorating that action, if for no other reason than to persuade the millions of Americans who have visited and will visit the city of Quebec that when their countrymen die on foreign soil they are not forgotten?

On the other hand, the monument in the Governor's Garden, the little park west of the Chateau Frontenac, is for both Wolfe and Montcalm, and it is inscribed: "Their courage gave them the same fate; history the same fame; posterity the same monument."

Quebec is full to the brim of interesting churches, other old buildings, and monuments. Free pamphlets from the Provincial Publicity people, or at your hotel, will identify

them. A look at the imposing Parliament Building, which
is just outside the city walls, will prove rewarding. There
are many fine hotels, tourist courts, and private rooms
available, but it would be far better to make reservations in
advance. If you have any special problem along that line,
write the Province of Quebec Provincial Publicity Bureau, Tourist Branch, 106 Grande-Allee, Quebec, or, in
New York, 48 Rockefeller Plaza. They may be able to
make recommendations. (Hotels: Chateau Frontenac,
Clarendon, St. Louis, St. Roch and Victoria.)

Just before I left Quebec it got around to approximately
the same day of the year, and almost the same kind of
night, as that on which Wolfe's men made their famous
ascent of the cliff to the Plains of Abraham. So I drove out
to the spot in a taxi and climbed up. I got wet, very
muddy, and a little scratched up, but it wasn't bad. Of
course I didn't have a long musket, a grenadier's hat, or a
knapsack with a Field Marshal's baton in it. And I had a
taxicab waiting, instead of the French, while all my firing
and falling back was done at a cozy tavern—the nearest
one.

From hearing the memories of Quebec's winter tourists,
it must be the happy get-togethers in the cocktail bars and
taverns, talking things over when recollections of the trail
are fresh, that each year brings them back. But the way I
look at it, there are bars closer at hand. Around Quebec
City you may also ski on the famous Valcartier slopes, curl,
see and play hockey, skate (both indoors and outdoors),
and take an old-fashioned sleigh ride. Item: plump girls
give off more warmth on sleigh rides, thin girls look better in ski clothes.

Now I was ready for the Gaspé tour.

It has become the custom among sophisticated authors
on tourist matters to give off with a raucous Bronx *viva* at

any section of the country the tourists frankly enjoy. But I still like the Gaspé tour. The Gaspé Peninsula is like a mittened left hand outlined by the ever-broadening St. Lawrence River, its gulf, and the Baie des Chaleurs. In the center there is a national park surrounded by huge forests. Only the sea-girt perimeter is inhabited, the road circling the coast, dipping into tiny fishing villages, climbing over towering headlands, affording magnificent views, and granting opportunity to savor life where the hand of time has been stayed.

Before leaving Quebec be sure to get the Publicity Bureau's Historic Guide to Gaspé, which will tell you something of each little town through which you'll pass; space limitations preclude our doing that. But whatever literature you read on these towns reveals obsession with church dates and characters, a subject you can't all be restricted to. The Gaspé tour doesn't begin until you reach Mont Joli, and you may decide to go down there by train and take the Gaspé Tours' four-day trip, for $85, which pays for everything except having your shoelaces pressed.

However, if you drive, you will take the ferry from Quebec across to Levis and then take Route 2 to Rivière du Loup, Route 10 from there to Ste. Flavie; and then Route 6 out on the Gaspé circle (which, however, you can take either way, clockwise or the reverse). The church at Levis, St. Joseph's, was fitted up as a hospital for Wolfe's wounded after the battle of the Plains of Abraham, then destroyed by fire in 1830. After Wolfe "wrote the book" on how to take Quebec, the British set up four forts here, three of which you may visit today. Nine miles away, at Beaumont, a mill built in 1733 has been converted into a museum, and the church, built the same year, displays interesting wood carvings. (A bit farther on you will be able to purchase exquisite carvings, unless, perhaps, you prefer to whittle your own.) St. Michel is noted for eel fishing, which hardly seems to go with the fact that it is also noted as a bathing beach. St. Vallier and Berthier also have fine beaches, and there are several small hotels and two tourist courts in the area.

Two workshops worthy of visiting may be found at St. Jean-Port-Joli. Eugene Leclerc builds fabulous little ships and the Bourgault brothers are decorative carvers. Also here is an interesting church, unchanged since 1770, and the grave of P. A. de Gaspé, author of *Les Anciens Canadiens*. After whirling through several resort villages you come to Rivière du Loup, where Champlain first shook hands with the tribe of Indians which gave the place its name. They say this tribe is now extinct, but I wouldn't want to bet on it. You roll out on Route 10 to Three Pistols (Trois-Pistoles) through Rimouske, which means "Land of the Moose," to Pointe-au-Père, where I, at least, was interested to learn that ocean liners stop and pick up the pilots who live in this town and know how to guide them to Quebec. And at Ste. Flavie (and we aren't half through our list of saints, yet) you meet Route 6, beginning of the Gaspé tour.

The regular trip started from the Hotel Commercial, Mont Joli, but I was taken only as far as Boule Rock Hotel, at Metis Beach, where I rested almost two days. The manager, a roly-poly fellow like myself, and jolly the same as all of us built that way, advertises that his place, achoo! is absolutely free of whatever it is that bothers hay-fever sufferers. I enjoyed my stay there, hiking along the beach with Miss Esther Taillon, a secretary or typist of the FBI in Washington, D.C., and young Alex Hislop temporarily took the place of my own three sons who, when we were down on the Mexican border, listened 'way past bedtime to stories of my skill and daring as an amateur bullfighter.

When our car showed up I was delighted to learn that the driver was Monsieur Guy d'Anjou, described by Claud Melançon as a very intelligent law student, and, I learned, not falsely depicted. As fellow passengers I had Monsieur d'Anjou's grandfather, an interested old codger who never tired of sightseeing, Bertram Berney, of Baltimore, friend of friends of mine, world-traveler and fellow *aficionado* of Mexico, and Raymond W. MacLaughlin, of the investment-banking business in Philadelphia. We were all, like our fellow-American, Bing Crosby (I was to run across his tracks later in the Rockies) grunt-and-groan-over-the-scenery men. D'Anjou would stop anywhere we liked, it was our party, and when we started finding stone bakeries on the lawns and salty old "French" fishermen, tiny stone villages up against leaning sails, dogs pulling milk carts, and exquisite views of the Shickshocks (Gaspé's extension of the Appalachians) well, it's a wonder we aren't still there.

We were absolutely compatible. No one mentioned a comparison to Maine or to any particular place in France. Each new thing we took up in wonder, in turn. Down by the huge cod-flaking boards we went, and into the interesting churches, the country stores, and even some of the homes, upon proper invitation. That night we stayed in the Hotel Bon Accueil at Rivière-Madeleine and ate fried codfish tongues. The place is owned by M. C. Berube and staffed by his innumerable daughters, all of them very pretty and oo-la-lahing all over the place. After dinner we played games and sang songs while one of the girls played the piano. They made us feel like members of the family who by just a lucky coincidence didn't have to wash or dry dishes.

"Be sure that you will get for your money," was one complete sentence in a Hotel Bon Accueil advertisement. (The name means "Hearthy" Welcome, the ad went on to explain.) But hospitality like that needs no English translation.

As we drove by, Blanchet's cabins, beyond Madeleine, looked comfortable, and, a little later, Godfray's Cabins, at the threshold of a sportsman's paradise. We overtook an Ohio car which had conked out. We pushed it up hills until we decided it wouldn't go, then drove ahead to send a garageman back. This sort of help from fellow *voyageurs* can be expected by you, too, should something untoward occur to the family ark. The Gaspésian Cabins looked all right at Anse-à-Valleau, and this whole countryside seemed just the place to take a new bride: plenty to see and exclaim about, take pictures of, walk to, and swim in; not too many people around and no dressing up for meals.

We lunched at the very fine Battery Park Hotel, Gaspé, and then went up to the monument which marks the spot believed consecrated by priests accompanying Jacques Cartier, when he came ashore and planted a cross in 1534. In two very vital ways, this is where Canada began.

Here it was that Cartier claimed the land for his French king, saying to hell with searching for India, this was going to be good enough for his men's grandchildren and it would be good enough for his men. After the religious ceremony was completed and he had impressed a few of the local Order of Redmen, Cartier started taking notes with which to excite the interest of the current Louis. As an explorer he was almost a carpetbagger. Leif Erickson had been Canada's first tourist. Then there had been the Cabot brothers, in 1497, only five years after Columbus set the vogue. But they went back to England (probably because there weren't any Lodges around to engage in conversation.) Next Gasper Cortereal, around 1500, made a visit, followed by Esteban Gomez, in 1525. But Cartier was the first to think of colonization.

Singularly enough, from this same harbor some 370 years later, descendants of the Cartier expedition and of the Indian reception party who met them were among the members of Canada's largest single expeditionary force, which sailed to sweep the Hun out of France. Then, in World War I, Canada assumed the stature of a nation.

The day I visited Gaspé there were toy white sails on the quiet waters, fleecy sheep in the meadows. Leaves were turning, and the geese and the tourists, in the main, were heading south.

Later we went to the fish hatchery and tried to appear interested in pisciculture, and so on around the incomparable coast to Perce, where, we are assured by the travel folders, "the tourist's dreams come true." At Mountain View Peak, just before we came down into the town, the manager told us Mrs. Eleanor Roosevelt had once stayed there, which, come to think of it, is a distinction all right, but nothing unique. (There is nothing to the rumor, however, that this very gracious lady's name and face is going to be put on St. Christopher's medals.)

As we drove up to our excellent hotel, Au Pic de l'Aurore, or Peak O'Dawn, we got our first closeup of the famous pierced rock which Cartier noted on his log some 414 years ago, although it was a bit different in shape then. Someone with nothing better to do has figured out that the portion of rock exposed above water weighs four million tons. And while Cartier didn't leave us any figures, we know the rock was larger then than now because some of the grandfathers of old-timers now living used to recall how part of it fell into the sea, making a bigger splash than the prize debutante of the New York season.

Sometimes at low tide one may walk the six hundred feet from the mainland to Perce Rock, crossing over a sandbar. But you are never able to go all the way around the rock on foot. The day may come, however, when some promoter will build a causeway out there and reproduce Mont St. Michel on this continent.

Nearby is Bonaventure Island, absolutely unique as a bird sanctuary. It looks like a huge whale about three miles offshore, and tens of thousands of gulls and gannets call it home. They take you around it in a boat as part of the Gaspé Tour.

There are some other excellent hotels at Perce, including the Normandie, Perce Rock House, Biard's Beach, Bleu-Blanc-Rouge, Le Nid du Corbeau, and The Three Sisters. Near by there is the most perfect little fishing village on the route, Anse-à-Beaufils, where your car winds in among the sails.

The remainder of the Gaspé tour is pretty much cut along the pattern previously delineated. Newport has an exceptional harbor, a slit between huge crags. Shigawake means "Japan" in Micmac, or "Land of the Rising Sun." New Carlisle's hotels looked good in passing (La Maison Blanche and New Carlisle) and the town is famed as a quiet summer resort on the "Warm Bay." St. Bonaventure is the Tour's dinner and overnight stop, at the Chateau Blanc, which is recommended. Only eight miles separates Maria and Carleton (Des Sables Rouges Hotel) the two towns named to honor Guy Carleton, who was made Lord Dorchester after his defeat of General Montgomery. Dorchester's wife was named Maria. But St. Omer, six miles farther on, is a much better place to spend your time and money, with its lovely beaches and drives. Pointe-à-la-Garde was named to honor the man who fought the last-guard land battle with the British at the end of their conquest, and just off Restigouche, fourteen miles farther on, was fought the last naval fight. The name of Restigouche establishes a bond between the modern American child and the savage Micmac, for it was their battlecry, meaning "disobey your father!"

At Matapedia's Hotel Restigouche, where the Gaspé Tours stop for lunch, the talk is all about salmon catching. They have a red-hot salmon-fishing club here and the members outdo one another ingeniously in getting to previously inaccessible fishing pools. Now up the beautiful Matapedia Valley, stopping at St. Moise to see the Renaissance-style church, and so to Mont Joli, or Pretty Hill, where we started.

There perhaps is nothing else in Quebec to compare with the Gaspé Tour, unless one speaks of the Saguenay River cruise. Every day, throughout the season, boats leave Quebec for the sail down the majestic St. Lawrence and up the turgid waters of the Saguenay, one of the largest tributaries of the Father of Canadian Streams. Murray Bay and Tadoussac, at the mouth of the Saguenay, are ports of call. The Saguenay, called the deepest river in the world, is dark and mysterious. The ship plows a black furrow as she threads through towering canyons which toss back the whistle's blast and, seen from the bow, seem to relent and let you pass, knot by knot. When you reach the twin climaxes of Cape Eternity and Cape Trinity nobody cheers. Everyone is too impressed. Here in the north is gold, but no one knows much about the section because very few people have explored it.

There are a few other Quebec roads which may be briefly described. For example, go northeast out of Montreal to Route 11, and into the winter-sports wonderland through Ste. Therese, St. Jerome, Shawbridge, Mont-Rolland, Ste. Adele, Val Morin, Ste.-Agathe-des-Montes (Hotel St. Vincent) and St. Jovite. This is the Mont-Tremblant area, where Joseph B. Ryan, the Philadelphia millionaire, holds forth amidst Swiss-style chalets renting at $7.00 a day and up. Mr. Ryan recently shared honors with his mountain in a *Saturday Evening Post* piece notable for its lovely color pictures.

Also Route 19 is good from Three Rivers to Grand Mère, about thirty miles, and Route 8 (with one bad section) from the Montreal area to Hull, some 123 miles. That relegates hundreds of secondary roads in the province to jeep travel. So we turn our attention to Ontario.

· 8 ·

Ontario, a Continent by Itself

BACK so long ago that Ohio State University had football teams able to trounce Michigan occasionally, I was a student there and counted among my journalistic friends Harry Keys, then with the *Columbus Citizen,* later famous cartoonist of *The Passing Show* for the Columbus (Ohio) *Sunday Dispatch.* Keys made a summer vacation trip to the Province of Ontario, fishing at Chaffey's Locks. Then he drew a full page showing the Duke of Wellington, fishermen, and the map of the province, and wrote a caption telling the story of the Rideau Canal, of Ontario.

"The War of 1812 left a bitterness that poisoned relations between Canada and the United States for many years. Fearing trouble in the future, the Duke of Wellington built the Rideau (pronounced Ree-do) Canal," Keys wrote.

"By connecting a string of lakes with canals and locks, a waterway was built from Ottawa to Kingston—thus making it unnecessary to transport troops and supplies up the St. Lawrence River, where ships could be fired upon from the United States shores—it cost the British Government four million dollars and it took five years to complete it.

"The waterway that was built to keep Americans from invading Canada has become a magnet to draw them northward in quest of vacations on beautiful lakes surrounded by pine forests and dotted with islands and there, Canadians, who were once afraid we'd come, are now glad to have us."

Mr. Keys packed much that is pertinent to any description of the Province of Ontario into that succinct caption. Ontario is glad to have you—welcomed between ten and eleven million tourists (estimated) last year. This, though Ontario is, to a certain extent, still fighting the war of 1812, being more British than the "Limehouse Blues" and burdening some visitors with an Etonian ennui as phony as a *Hasty Pudding* chorus line.

Last year more than 60 per cent of Canada's tourist revenue is supposed to have entered through customs ports in this province (they say 55,000,000 people live within a day's travel of Toronto, and that city makes a definite bid for American conventions on the ground that it is "on the ground" between New York and Chicago, which is true). Ontario has literally everything for the tourist, with 2,000 miles of fresh-water shore line on four of the five Great Lakes tossed into the picture instead of the usual salt water coast line, and 600 miles of salt-water shore line on Hudson Bay. Ontario is "foreign," as England is "foreign," and within her far-flung boundaries there are bustling modern cities, mighty rivers, sleepy villages, busy mining towns, and, to the north, the vast silences of primeval forests—in short, the topography and climate of a whole continent, rather than just a province. And Ontario is promotion-minded—quite an item—with exactly the right people doing the work.

Ontario is the second largest Canadian province, slightly less than twice the size of Texas, and with one-third of Canada's population. But what is more important, it is located in the center of the nation, with good soil, power potentialities, and all the rest of nature's best. So that with the addition of a sensible, hard-working, conservative citizenry, the picture is complete. Ontario is first in numbers, wealth, industry, agriculture, and progress in the nation.

The southern tip of the province has a climate similar to that of northern New York, while in the extreme north they've known snow in July. More than 80 per cent of the province lies south of the isotherm of 60 degrees Fahrenheit (mean July temperature), which sounds good but means it can get damned cold. And Ontario has a density of only ten persons to a square mile, leaving lots of room to play and produce and grow, but you won't believe that when you first enter from the United States.

Take a look at Ontario's shape on the map. Tilt it slightly and use your imagination. It looks like a headless, hefty, muscle-bound mermaid. All her population has gone to her flippers.

If you cross over at Detroit, Buffalo, or Cornwall you'll get the determined impression that Ontario is made up of good roads, big business, smartly turned-out towns reflecting a fine balance between industry and agriculture, high tension lines, booster clubs and people almost the same as back home in the United States. Much of that summation is true.

Over masses of chicken à la king, apparently prepared by paper hangers and followed by slabs of something between sheets of cardboard but labeled "apple pie," orators on both sides of the Canada-United States line have sounded off for years about the similarity between the two peoples. The fact is that Canadians are individual, not too much like either the British or the Americans.

Those who talk about a common language are ignoring an essential and vital fact. Canada is bilingual. It has two official languages, French and English.

A Canadian does not take a vacation; he takes a holiday. He posts a letter; he doesn't mail it. He goes into the bush, not into the northwoods. He lies about catching a three-pound trout, not a twelve-incher. He rarely does his buying in a store, he goes to a shop. The things which keep up his trousers are braces, not suspenders; crackers are biscuits and what Americans call Canadian bacon is back bacon to a Canadian. When you ask a Canadian a question which he muffs he says, "Eh?" In the mass this sounds like a group of sparrows quarreling among the eaves. It contrasts strongly with the American "Huh?" which has the blunt finality of an overfed woman plopping her chassis into a subway seat.

All postage stamps, all paper money, and all official documents are printed in both French and English; the stamps say "Postes" and "Postage." The paper money reads "Five Dollars" and "Cinq Dollars."

Although he likes corn on the cob, baseball, and Rita Hayworth, the Canadian is a different breed of human from the American. He is cautious, quiet, and, generally speaking, an introvert by nature as well as by habit. Of course these are general remarks, and the western Canadian differs, radically, from the others. But that the composite Canadian is naturally conservative there can be little doubt. Life is, of course, more rugged in this generally colder country, and all of you are familiar with the difference this makes in our own country—between, say, a Texan and a Vermonter. Again speaking generally, people tend to reflect the climate they live in, all over the world, in their outward selves or in the first impressions they impart. Thus you will discover few men in Canada cavorting in public in baggy red trousers, crimson fezzes, and other varieties of peacock attire, and behaving in the fashion of suspended adolescence, unless they are visiting Americans in convention. Some Canadians, it is true, belong to Shrines and others to lodges whose rules require that they shall wear shredded cocoanut on their hats. But they confine their activities to quarters, in the main. There are excep-

tions. Church services and St. Jean Baptiste parades sometimes bring out male plumage, but those events demand
decorum, so all is well. The normal Canadian has a holy
terror of wearing anything but the conventional garb of
business; it is usually as much as a wife can do to get
hubby into a dress suit, while only a woman with a whim
of iron can attend a masquerade ball accompanied by her
life-escort. You can imagine how distressed the Canadian is
to read of the antics of the Doukhobors—queer birds who
doff all their feathers when they have a point to make with
the Canadian government.

This conservatism of the Canadian is not due to an English background. Perhaps nowhere on earth can you find
another people who are as almost completely impervious
to propaganda as are Canadians. They are bombarded by
American magazines, books, radio shows, and movies.
They actually have no movies (Canadian produced), of their
own. Yet they are not drastically influenced. They are
bombarded simultaneously by lecturers, radio broadcasts,
and political and legal traditions from the British Isles.
Yet they aren't British. They have successfully withstood
these influences, constant and strong as they are, and have
achieved a character that is different from either the American or the British. But the people in the Ontario areas
nearest the United States were, in great part, United Empire Loyalists who wanted to imitate and even reproduce
England. They built a London (on its Thames), a Stratford (with its Avon and near-by Shakespeare), a Windsor,
Chatham, Colchester, Woodstock, Highgate, Lambeth, and
Charing Cross. (They also have their Waterloo.)

They built well. Now the giant Ontario Hydroelectric
Power Commission is doing exciting things. Already electric power has mightily helped Ontario, to the point where
she is producing more than half of Canada's consumer

goods. They are also harnessing nature in the north, building huge dams, and entire towns to order. When we start touring the province we'll describe such a town.

Ontarians travel more, both inside Canada and out, than other Canadians; have more telephones, read more, see more movies, advertise more, and see more foreign tourists. Yet, they are accused by other Canadians of being insular. Every commentator notes this but I believe it greatly overemphasized. I found Ontarians friendly, well informed, interested in their work, and, like Americans, unable to relax. They also have almost identical forms of play with their neighbors in "the States," except they concentrate a little less on the architecture of a dry martini as the noblest work of man. There are only a few cocktail lounges in an area four times the size of England.

When you talk about Canada being the land of the future you must include Ontario and the West Coast. They have a future, along with the North Country and our Alaska. They aren't afraid to face it and they're advertising in England for immigrants to come share it. Who knows, the tide of immigration may some day shift from the United States to Canada!

Enter Ontario by air, rail, ship, ferry, or bridge. You can fly Canadian Colonial from New York to Montreal, and there pick up Trans-Canada for scheduled stops such as Toronto or Ottawa, or take Trans-Canada from New York to Toronto (and make it in two hours—that convention come-on again). Going by rail from Chicago you have a choice of the Grand Trunk or the Michigan Central (with Canadian Pacific connections); from New York you would go via Montreal; and from Buffalo, to Toronto and thence to your destination. Canadian National Railways operates boats for regular lake passenger trips, and their schedules may be obtained by writing them at Montreal.

There are at least eleven ferries leading into the province and there are the following bridges: Ambassador Bridge, Detroit to Windsor; Blue Water Highway Bridge, Port Huron to Sarnia; Roosevelt Bridge, Roosevelttown to Cornwall; Thousand Islands Bridge from near Clayton to near Rockport; Peace Bridge, Buffalo to Fort Erie, Lewiston to Queenston.

You can also fly your own airplane in, if you land at a customs port or outport, and give them several hours' notice beforehand that you are coming. Lower Ontario is also practical for the hiker or bicyclist, as few Canadian provinces are. Towns are so close together that several of my friends say they have enjoyed doing it on foot. In this motorized age it is considered eccentric to walk, but then not more so than indulgence in half a dozen other sensible habits. For a walking tour you'll need to know in detail about places to stay, because if suggested places have no vacancies you won't be able to breeze on lightheartedly until you discover a room. Write for the pamphlet *Where to Stay in Ontario*, Department of Travel and Publicity, Parliament Buildings, Toronto 2, Ontario. (If flying your own plane, ask also for *Flying Facts About Ontario*.)

Going right to the heart of things Canadian, we enter at Buffalo and take the beautiful Queen Elizabeth Way, a super-road, to Toronto. A hop and skip to your right is Queenston, one of the best-guarded places in the nation in wartime, because it is the heart of the heart, the power center for that great production area of lower Ontario. Niagara's force runs the great dynamos. And, as has been pointed out very often, one successful saboteur could have blown up these great works, thus pulling the switch on the war effort. Now, with new power available, that wouldn't be so easy. Since power developed here is plentiful and cheap, the Queen Elizabeth Way is lighted incandescently, a city street stretching ninety miles. Night driving on it is about a half safer than on ordinary roads, owing to the divided lanes of traffic and the screening out, with shrubbery, of approaching lights. This is the great Niagara Peninsula, blossom bower bisected by the famous Welland Canal, key link in the great Seaway which will one day allow big ships passage between the lakes. This will bypass Niagara, which no one has navigated successfully in anything bigger than a barrel. Some rather large ships use the Welland Canal, and it is almost unbelievable to see them climbing hills by means of locks.

The Queen Elizabeth Way takes you through St. Catherine's and Hamilton, the main traffic transitway and an important city. (Royal Connaught, King George, Waldorf and Windsor Hotels; rates, a trifle higher than we've noted as an average.)

From Windsor to Toronto, you'd probably select Route 2. But down here in what is known as the sunparlor of the province, there are some things worth seeing. Along Route 18, take a quick drive down to see Fort Malden at Amherstburg, dating back to the name-calling of 1812. A little farther on is Jack Miner's Bird Sanctuary, which is fine, if you are fond of our feathered friends. Point Pelee National Park and Rondeau Provincial Park, a bit farther on, are choice spots for summer vacationists, especially trailerites. The bathing is unexcelled; on cool white beaches the government has set aside fully equipped camping spots, at low rentals, and if you get enthused to that point, you may even lease your own land at $25 a year and build a cottage. (There is a great deal of that in Ontario, and it's a poor Ontario addict who hasn't his own island off somewhere, renting at a token price annually.)

To explore along the north shore are miles and miles of unexcelled Lake Erie beaches, the Houghton Sand Hills,

and thirty-mile-long Long Point jutting across the Lake.
Port Stanley (Orion and New Biltmore Hotels, Hillcrest
Inn) and Crystal Beach (Park Teal's and Martinell Hotels)
are full-blown resort towns.

But, if you haven't taken this diversion off Route 2,
you'll proceed to Chatham (here the hotels include the
William Pitt, Chatham, Rankin, and Canadian Pacific
Railways) from whence John Brown's soul first marched.
At King and Adelaide Streets there's a plaque on his house,
where he and cohorts plotted against the United States
Government. On to Thamesville, turn left twelve miles to
Dresden, and near by is Uncle Tom's grave—yes, the Uncle
Tom of the famous novel, that corny classic by Harriet
Beecher Stowe which did so much to dramatize the moral
issues of human slavery. Mrs. Stowe visited Uncle Tom
(the Reverend Josiah Henson) here after he had escaped
by the Underground Railroad, for which the Chatham
area was the end of the line and you needed no transfer for
freedom. Dresden's Horticultural Society beautified Uncle
Tom's grave last year.

You drive through model villages and small cities, laid
out almost too perfectly, and come to London (London,
Belvedere, and Fraser Hotels) which is a fairly good-sized
city, with its Piccadilly and Pall Mall and Cheapside.
London boasts the famous University of Western Ontario.
Windbreakers and hedgerows give you that authentic
taste of the English countryside through Woodstock and
Paris. Route 2 takes you to Brantford, where it is possible
to see the actual house in which Alexander Graham Bell
invented the telephone; there's a memorial near by. Also
in the neighborhood there's an Indian reservation, and
the ramshackle wooden Church of the Mohawks. This is
the Valley of the Grand River, which many tourists "do"
from Port Maitland, on Lake Erie, to Georgian Bay. This

was a favorite canoe trip for Six Nations braves on week ends. For Toronto you would, of course, continue east on Route 99 to Hamilton and there take either Route 5 or the Queen Elizabeth Way.

From Sarnia, opposite Port Huron, the famous Blue Water Highway, Number 21, runs north to adventure and relaxation, skirting the shores of Lake Huron to Southampton. Kettle Point, just outside Sarnia, boasts of unusual rock formations and fossils. There is good fishing all along here as you drive through Ipperwash Park and on to Grand Bend, where a gal has ten times the chances for a date in the summer as in the winter. The population jumps tenfold with the warm weather. (Hotels: Bremmer, or Imperial, $4.00 per day and up, American plan; and Lakeview House.)

At Goderich (Park House and Sunset Hotel), Inverhuron and Port Elgin (the Maples, Royal Princess Lodge, Sunset Lodge) Lake Huron's waters are the attraction, although there are numerous inland streams presenting possibilities to the fisherman. Beyond Southampton (Highland, MacKenzies, and Saugeen Cabins), at the northern end of the Blue Water Highway, King's Highway Number 6 branches off to the interesting Bruce Peninsula, and eventually to the Manitoulin Island ferry. Manitoulin is reputedly the world's largest fresh-water island. The name means "Home of the Great Spirit," and you'll agree if it was good enough for the Great Spirit it's good enough for you: ninety-nine miles of vacationland, terrific bass fishing, private coves for bathing, grand little yacht harbors, Indian villages, and the white mountains of La Cloche. This is tops! (Manitowaning Lodge, at Manitowaning, $35 per week, and up.) Franklin Delano Roosevelt fished McGregor Bay, just north of the eastern end of the island, prior to the Quebec Conference.

If you haven't Manitoulin in mind, Route 21 continues on to connect with Route 26 for the Georgian Bay country, and Huronia. Near Midland, on Route 27 on the bank of the Wye, they hope to have historic Fort Ste. Marie, one of the most important historic ruins in America, restored by 1949. This will be the three-hundredth anniversary of the martyrdom of four Jesuit priests during the Iroquois obliteration of the fort. Near by, at the junction of Routes 11 and 12, is Orillia, a fine little resort town with thirteen miles of lake shore line inside its city limits. In that neighborhood a man can sometimes catch a muskie two-thirds his own size. This is all part of Huronia, and the excavations going on near here aim to restore the largest of the ancient Huron towns, Cahaigue. Champlain visited this area while egging the Hurons on to take the Iroquois' scalps, and a monument has been erected to commemorate sanguinary campfires. Orillia has a municipally operated camp for trailerites and tenters and thirty-four tourist camps and motels, including the De Lux Cabins, Orillia Log Cabins, and Rustic Rest. From there, take Route 11 south eighty-five miles to Toronto, Queen City of Canada.

· 9 ·

Toronto: Anthill with a Purpose

Toronto, as Malcom MacDonald once said, is a million people hidden in a forest. It is also the home of the most powerful fresh-water yacht club in the world and of the tallest office building and the largest hotel in the British Empire. It is the industrial nerve center of the nation, leading the world as a mining exchange. Now that you can buy cocktails at the Royal York Hotel, and seats on Toronto's stock exchange sell sometimes as high as $200,000, the town is growing up and you begin to get the pulse-beat of a city out of it, which is more than you can say for many a place with a million people bustling about. There is nothing too sophisticated about this observation. Toronto is inhabited by rockbound people; it takes some who want to build on the sands to make a city. All work and no obvious place to play makes Toronto—almost.

What goes on in Toronto? Lots of hard work, respect for and fear of the boss, a great community-wide love of the solid and the permanent, as reflected in the law that you can't build a wooden building. Must be brick or stone. Not much union organizing, and that done in fear and trembling. Down in the dour Parliament Building there is solemn piety as they enact high tariffs against fellow-Canadians. And perhaps this is revealing: There are more automobiles in the city of Toronto than in the entire Province of Quebec. A love for money as the stuff which commands respect, such as I have never seen anywhere else on this globe.

Toronto is a city where things happen, and I can never think of it as a place to relax or see things. It is an anthill with a purpose. I sat in the lobby of the palatial Royal York Hotel and tried to sum things up after I had been in the city a few days. That industrialist laughing over there behind his fat cigar: Surely he has just discovered a way to dispense with a tenth of his employees. The doctor hurrying through the lobby—it must be a matter of life and death. The shy young man biting his nails is mustering up his nerve for the first day on a new job. Who is relaxing? The too obvious answer: not anyone.

But that, I learned, is definitely not the fact. There are fourteen miles of frontage on the great inland sea of Lake Ontario, and nine of those miles are fine beaches. The entire district on the east side of the city is known as "The Beaches." No cars are allowed on Toronto Island, but one can get about easily by bicycle and trams. Here is a heaven of hamburger, soda water, and bathing girls. In town there are excellent dance bands playing at lunch and dinner. Toronto is a red-hot hockey town and a new star can cause a crowd to collect the way Babe Ruth used to gather them around him on Broadway. And there is a unique Mardi Gras on ice, the Toronto Skating Club Show. The curlers are among the best in the nation, and if an American wishes to see something interesting he should catch a "bonspiel," the "finals" of this grand Caledonian sport of stone and broom. There are fireworks on Queen Victoria's birthday, there is the King's Plate in May, and there are always the movies—made in Hollywood. Besides all this there are golf, boating, tennis, badminton—and culture. Toronto goes in for culture in a big way. It's the Toronto Symphony Orchestra in winter and the Toronto Philharmonic Orchestra in summer, both very much worth while, sometimes featuring famous guest conductors and well-known opera and radio stars.

Thousands of people crowd their way into the Royal Ontario Museum, where I found the Chinese section the best I had ever seen; and into the Toronto Art Gallery, simply overflowing with masterpieces.

Toronto gave the world a unique set of painters known as the "Group of Seven." Their work was original and had an influence on other native artists. Mary Pickford was born in this city. Franklin Davey McDowell, famous author of *The Champlain Road* (it would make a fine movie) and other works, lives and works there. I had lunch with him and he honored me with a dinner party at the Royal York, with more than half the literary lights of that section of the Dominion attending. Someone brought up the inevitable: "What's the matter with Canadian writers, that there aren't more of them, and that you don't hear more about them all over the world?" There didn't seem to be a satisfactory answer given then and I haven't read one, but if I were guessing I'd say it is because the rewards are too uncertain and because of the habits of the Canadian readers. Written by a Canadian? Then, they say, it can't be good.

In company with Miss Mary Ainslee, gifted and charming writer of pamphlets, I saw the town and checked the restaurants. Because Miss Ainslee is with a government bureau, I want it understood that these are my own selections: Winston Theatre Grill, 120 King Street, West, to be highly recommended; Club Norman, 12 Adelaide Street, East, Toronto's outstanding bar and night club, with good food, good floor show and atmosphere; Queen Elizabeth Lodge, Queen Elizabeth Way at Port Credit Road, excellent food served in exceptionally interesting bucolic surroundings; Guild of All Arts, Scarborough, a country inn, excellent; Bryan's Lobster Villa, 528 Lakeshore Road, Mimico (besides the lobster they have steak); King Edward Hotel, 37 King Street, East, and Royal York Hotel, 100 Front Street, West, both downtown, very swank, with good food, supper dancing and "the works"; Stoodleigh Restaurant, 80 King Street, very attractive English-style dining room, superior home-cooked food; Angeleos Tavern, 144 Chestnut Street, a popular Italian restaurant; Little Bit of Denmark, 720 Bay Street, which is a little bit of all right; Lachaumière, 77 Charles Street, East, authentic in every way; Maison Doré, 38 Asquith Avenue, very small but another interesting French restaurant; Old Mill, for many years one of the city's outstanding places to eat and dance.

I think the most interesting tourist sights are a fort, a castle with a remarkable story behind it, and a statue to the guy who invented Sunday schools, Robert Raikes. The fort is York, erected in 1794 by General John Graves Simcoe, the Lieutenant Governor of Ontario, on the site of an old French fort and trading post "at the portage at Toronto, favorite meeting site of the Hurons." Today the historic spot is almost surrounded by railroad yards, which make it slightly harder to get to than in the times when it underwent its one battle, scars of which still show. (Drive down Garrison Road, which begins just west of the armories, which are *near* Strachan Avenue.)

On April 17, 1813, the fort capitulated to Americans who had landed near where the Sunnyside Amusement Park now is. As American troops marched into the fort, the powder magazine blew up, killing American General Zebulon Pike, some of his men, and some Canadians. The American troops reasoned that since the magazine hadn't blown up before, but just at that particular moment, there was something suspicious about it. So they burned the Parliament Building of the province, which later brought retaliation by British troops, who burned our President's residence at Washington. The scars were painted over with white paint—that's how our White House got its name. Happily the real scars of those days have long since disappeared, and the old fort is a symbol to remind us that we need tolerance on both sides, of how lucky we are that we have it.

The second biggest tourist attraction stemmed from the baronial moods of the late Sir Henry Pellatt, the sort of a chap who would never order a hamburger sandwich when he got hungry—he'd buy a restaurant. He acted just like a Billy Rose with a billion dollars. So when he wanted a modest place to lay his head he took a convenient hill-top which he happened to own, sent to Scotland for an army of masons, and kept them at work a year on the garden wall alone. His Castle Loma had turrets three hundred feet above the street level, which is as high as a thirty-story skyscraper; all his bathtubs had golden faucets; his kitchen was big enough to feed a regiment at a time; the library could accommodate 100,000 books; and from the basement a tunnel, wide enough to drive a car through, went under the street six hundred feet to the stables, where every horse had a Spanish-mahogany stall with bronze fittings. The Castle had a swimming pool, billiard rooms, bowling alley, two-hundred-foot rifle range, and a secret staircase from the library to the room above. The works cost $3,000,000 and was never finished even then.

Sir Hank sent The Queen's Own Bugle Band at his own expense to the coronation of Edward VII. When he died he was buried most impressively (I've read the accounts), after which people discovered he hadn't even a tired es-cudo left to his name. But what of it? His magnificent gestures must have inspired some persons in this unimaginative old world, which insists upon trying to reduce the human race to a uniform, colorless, tasteless, jelly mass. Now the city of Toronto, which was amused and amazed into lifting an eyebrow at Pellatt's Folly, owns the joint and heralds it as "Toronto's Fairy Castle." For a small fee you can see it by day or dance in it by night. But the pay-off in this story came after the war when it was revealed that as the thousands rubbernecked and jitterbugged through the building, scientists and workmen turned out a "top secret" submarine detection device—in the basement! This was an "actual demonstration of that old fiction idea that the best place to hide something is in the public eye," said George Rogers, editor of the *Toronto Star Weekly*, who told me the story and gave me the files to check it.

A city of innumerable churches, site of the only monument to the gent who dreamed up Sunday school, it is only natural that Toronto call off her National Exhibition each Sunday during its two weeks' run. Even the impressive Princes' Gates to the Canadian National Exhibition Park (the oldest *permanent* exhibition) give an air of solidity. But you'll admire the exposition if your visit takes place during the latter part of August or the first of September. And in keeping with this solidity, this attempt to regulate, which is in the very air in Toronto, it is noteworthy that the idea for standard time, which sets the watches of the world, was given out by Sir Sandford Fleming while in this city. You'll find a memorial tablet at 58 Richmond Street, East. Elsewhere about the city there are statues and memorials, and one of them, in the water basin before which children romp, is to the Samuel Adams of Canada, William Lyon Mackenzie, who did much good for Canadian democracy with his bloodless revolution: whether

Canada could have secured more democracy more quickly
in some other way depends upon how you look at it. This
memorial to the grandfather of Mackenzie King, the man
everyone had begun to believe was the perpetual prime
minister, is to be found on the west side of the Parliament
Buildings.

And so with a very respectful bow from the waist (one
would never *think* of anything else for the thoroughly
respectable, masculine, my, what-will-people-think! city)
we continue touring. We take familiar Route 2 past fine
towns good for lakeside bathing, and Trenton, where begins the Trent Waterway, a smooth-water highway running ribbon-like across one of the loveliest vacation districts
in Canada. Those among you with yachts or canoes pick
up here. The canal from Trenton to Peterborough will
take boats of eight-foot draft, but the way is clear for two
hundred miles, to Swift Rapids, for craft drawing only
six feet. And from there on to the sparkling whitecaps of
Georgian Bay there are two marine railways, smallest links
in the chain, which whittle down craft going that far to
forty-foot draft, twenty tons of weight.

In 1615 Champlain traveled the Trent, and from that
time on this natural "canal" between borders decked with
groves and shrubbery has been a favorite. But now, at
stupendous cost, portages around rapids and falls have
been eliminated. The entire system is so well regulated
that there are no great rises and falls due to rains or
droughts. Trenton, where we start, is famed for Cheddar
cheese; and Hay Bay, near by, for leaping muskies. Now
your boat goes through rich farming country, then rough
lands which must recall Scotland to the settlers from there,
and the locks at Campbellford and Healey Falls. You'll
wish you were a painter to catch the scenes between Healey
and Trent Bridge, twelve lovely miles.

Rice Lake is your entranceway to Bright Waters and Happy Lands, which actually is the translation for the name, Kawarthas, and couldn't be better for a vacation description. There are fifteen of these lakes. On Rice Lake, at the village of Hiawatha, are Indians who have an easy thing of it. They sold their land for $3,000 yearly to be paid the heads of families, and now the papas get $15 or so apiece. From Rice Lake you go on to the Otonabee, to the highest hydraulic lift lock in the world at Peterborough, and then to Lakefield, where they took the big log boom out of the water after sixty years and cut it up into fine new lumber.

Then comes Young's Point, one of the oldest and most popular summer colonies; Lovesick Lake, where Ogama and Manita drowned in each other's arms because they couldn't have each other, a new plot if I ever heard one; and, from Katchewanooka Lake and through Stony Lake, an unbelievable Venice-in-the-wilderness effect due to little cottages being built on innumerable tiny islands. A white church sits at a narrow passageway between two rocks indelicately called Hell's Gate. In summer everyone goes to church in his motorboat, stepping from the nether regions of the gate to the quiet waters of the bay and heavenly hope. At Burleigh Falls there is good fishing and Forest Hill Lodge ($4.50 a day and up, American plan) and the Park Hotel. Indian guides are available from the Curve Lake reservation. Buckhorn and Chemong Lake have floating pontoon bridges which sink slightly ahead of you as you drive over. When winter ice begins to break up around these bridges the chains are broken and the bridges go out, to be picked up and mended later. While the bridges are being mended—what a sight!—floating detours are placed around the floating span. And when craft

have to pass through the floating bridge? Oh, they float
through a swing bridge suspended over it.

Hunting is so good around Bobcaygeon that they tell
scandalously extravagant stories about it. (Locust Lodge,
Pine Ridge Lodge, and others.) Sturgeon Lake is where
Ogama and Manita, the two Indian hepcats mentioned
above, are buried, and there is something about the atmosphere here which seems to make the farther shores
float in tears. Rosedale is pretty. Balsam Lake is where
the waters of the Trent System appear to bulge upward.
Since it is the highest point, either way is downstream.
The channel leads down to Coboconk, or Chuckling
Waters, which must represent light wine, since Giggle
Water stands for whisky. And so it goes, on through Kirk-
field's great hydraulic lift lock, into Lake Simcoe, a minor-
league pool to the Great Lakes, but big leagues in fishing.
Winters find the lake dotted with fishermen's shacks. Thus
to Orillia, which has been previously described, and farther on, the Severn River section, which runs through
small farms and resorts so idyllic that it is like a canal trip
in Old France. Beyond Sparrow Lake the scenery is wilder,
the hills higher, and the way running sometimes between
rock walls. Here are Ragged Rapids, Pretty Channel, and
Go Home Bay. Here are the marine railways and finally
Georgian Bay's glittering mercury-like surface. Southward
lies Victoria Harbor, Port McNicoll, and Midland. Northward is Beausoleil, Island of Beautiful Sunshine. Dead
ahead are the wind-swept Thirty Thousand Islands, the
Giant's Tomb, and the Flower Pot Islands, where the trees
are bent by the winds. And thus one could go on to Manitoulin Island, or anywhere in the Great Lakes.

Coming back to Route 2 on our way to Ottawa, it is a
short ride through Belleville to the ancient town of Kingston, where we leave the Toronto to Montreal road to cut

up through the lake country. Not far from Kingston, along the St. Lawrence River, is the bird sanctuary and haven for all things romantic, of Wallace Havelock Robb, Canadian nature poet. Robb has a bell which can be heard seven miles and was cast in England to honor an Indian poet; he also has a collection of stones he found in the neighborhood and which may prove the earlier existence of a lost race. Kingston, once capital of the nation, is one of its oldest cities. Among the points of interest there: A Martello tower, now a museum; the Royal Military College, Canada's West Point; old Fort Frederick, inside the military college grounds, now a weapons display house; Fort Henry, built to keep the Americans away, and attracting them now as tourists. The old fort never had to be used; good thing, too, say the local crackerbarrel strategists, 'cuz the danged thing's facing the wrong way!

Let's take the Rideau to Ottawa, and even if you drive your car there this water trip will tell the story of the region. Kingston Mills, six miles above the city, has the first locks and is the site of the first blockhouse; you'll recall the Iron Duke had the plan that the Rideau should be built so troops could be brought to the Kingston area without being under fire from the American side of the St. Lawrence. These blockhouses were for defense in depth of his waterways communications. Above here is an area of what would be called swamps anywhere else, but which the British called "Drowned Lands," so that's different. Just past Brewer's Mills Lock there's a profile carved by nature on the rock, and they say it looks just like the Duke of Wellington. At the entrance to Cranberry Lake it is possible to begin the portages to Battersea, an attractive summer colony. (Erwell Manor, Granite House, and Loughboro Inn.) The main route, however, is straight ahead to Brass Point, Whitefish Lake (where you may go down

Morton Bay to Morton Creek through wonderful scenery rivaling the upper Saguenay), and Jones' Falls, a very pretty place where the ghosts of dead British soldiers dig for their pay. The same is true at Foster's at the entrance to Lake Opinicon, and in this place there's supposed to be an entire keg of money buried to make the digging worth while.

Almost anywhere on the lake you may see a boat full of ghosts moving silently along without paddle or propeller, to vanish if a single noise is heard. At Chaffey's Locks is the only blockhouse which ever was menaced by an "enemy." Loyal Canadians mustered in it to defend the locks and other works during the unrest associated with the Rebels of Upper Canada, in 1838. You go on to Clear Lake, Newboro Lake, then Upper Rideau Lake, highest in the chain, and from Big Rideau a number of routes are opened up. Those who have time for a side excursion may run down to Portland. The main route runs on to Poonamalie, which got that fancy name because it reminded a British officer of India: the shadow-stripes thrown across the trails by light trees resemble the tiger bamboo out there. You can reproduce this effect in your photographs.

But the high point of the trip is Smith's Falls. Tie the boat up right in the center of the town and step through green lawns to do your shopping. The next town is Merrickville, site of the largest blockhouse on the route, and of the most amusing anecdote concerning the canal. Back in 1831 the government finished the canal, at a cost of millions, and Mr. Merrick decided to repair his mill, so he dammed the river and the government did without its canal until he finished, months later. Burritt's Rapids was founded by Colonel Stephen Burritt, who had spent seven years with the famous Roger's Rangers and was a cousin of the blacksmith in Longfellow's poem. Below here for twenty-six miles there are no locks, but there is beautiful scenery. And now take the Rideau River to Hogsback Lock, named after the large boulders in the stream. Thus you go on into the heart of Ottawa, through landscaped banks and extensive groves, the unique way to enter. You could actually get out of your craft at the Bank Street Bridge, take a few steps and catch a streetcar or taxi for anywhere in the capital.

· 10 ·

Ottawa, the Memorial City

OTTAWA almost perfectly reflects the tempo, greatness, mood, and sacrifices of the nation. Unless you are one of those who enjoys gawking at lawmakers, there are not many of the usual attractions here for tourists. But a quiet, exceedingly impressive stay in very good hotels, pleasant drives along three pleasant rivers, and unexcelled views of Victorian Gothic architecture set against verdant hills, can be had in Ottawa.

Champlain, that indefatigable traveler, first saw the site, stopping in 1613 to admire its promontories and seething waterfalls, and even today both native and stranger will come to a halt in the Plaza, at this same spot, just above the Rideau Canal west of the imposing Canadian National Railways' hotel, Chateau Laurier, to revel in this vista. The Chateau seems to be a part of the memorial city of Ottawa, fitting it even better than the Chateau Frontenac fits Quebec, which is highest praise for Canadian National Railways' architects and hotel management. (The rates are not low, however: $5.00 and up, for a single, European plan. Other hotels: Lord Elgin, Genosha, and Cadillac.) Don't miss the heroic statuary to Canadian dead, in and about government buildings.

From the capital you may swing around the edges of the province by taking Route 17 to the east through Rockland (Rockland and King George Hotels), and Route 34 at Hawkesbury; by turning right at Lancaster, you get back on Route 2, which then will take you along the St.

116

Lawrence and through such famous towns as Cornwall, settled by United Empire Loyalists (Cornwallis and King George Hotels), and Prescott, where Fort Wellington still shows War of 1812 battle scars. This fort was rebuilt in 1837 and was the rallying point for Canadians who, at a windmill near by, defeated the last armed invaders of their country. Nils von Schoultz, a young Pole living in the United States, had recruited Americans to join rebelling Canadians and free them from the tyranny of British rule of those days. He was the last of a long line of people from the United States to overestimate the willingness of Canadians to give up what they have.

This is all good fishing territory. Next comes Brockville, closest point on the Canadian border to New York City (Manitonna and Grand Central Hotels) and Gananoque, place of health, and its ferry and near-by bridge. You are then back at Kingston, where we previously had started the Rideau Canal trip.

Between Kingston and Belleville, Route 41 straight north takes you into the lesser known Land O'Lakes, which is prime fishing country. There are a thousand bodies of water; big bass in Mazinaw and Weslemkoon; lots of things to see around Kaladar, Cloyne, and Fernleigh; and Bon Echo, the hunk of rock and dirt which is known as Canada's Gibraltar, so of course they'll have to name an insurance company after it. Follow King's Highway 62 or 41 to Route 60, which runs along the southern area of Algonquin Park, for more scenery and piscatorial satisfaction.

Route 17 out of Ottawa toward the north and west is fine all the way to Chalk River, and not bad all the way, hundreds of miles, to the Sault Ste. Marie country between Lakes Superior and Huron. You follow the course of the Ottawa River for the first part of the journey, reversing the route followed by the old French fur traders who came out of the northwest country by way of Ottawa headed for the *vin et femmes blancs* of Montreal. At Des Joachim the Hydro people are building one of the largest dams since Niagara, to back up water for seventy-eight miles (all the way to Mattawa) and supply electric energy at the rate of 400,000 horsepower a year to the people of the province within four years. An entire city is set up in Ontario and another in Quebec province. Both the highway and the railroad must be moved, but it's all part of the restless, progressive spirit of the producing heart of Canada.

A short drive farther on and you arrive on the fringes of Lake Nipissing. Turn left on Route 11 a short distance if you want to see Callander, home of the well-publicized quintuplets. I felt their novelty had been used up, so I didn't bother to interview them for you. One of these days they'll be getting married, and I'll wager that at least two of them will take the vows on the same day.

There is an old wheeze about the fellow who claimed to be an actor: he ran for the doctor in *The Birth of a Nation*. Arling Clark, a friend of mine who owns and operates a fishing camp on Sandy Island, Lake Nipissing, is almost a like candidate for an actor's Oscar. He ran for Doctor Dafoe when the quints were on their way. Arling Clark's Camp is on the north shore, a nice place to land an amphibious plane and fish or just swim and get away from everything and almost everybody. Arling puts six persons in a cabin at a rental of $4.00 a day for the cabin (cabins have only outside toilets). You bring your own food and cook it, buying ice and firewood from the Clarks. At Sturgeon, houseboats may be chartered and towed to the better fishing grounds.

North Bay is another one of those travel hubs with which we've had to concern ourselves. (Empire and Continental Hotels, Pine Point Log Cabins, and several others.) South on excellent King's Highway 11 you may drive easily to Bracebridge, and if you want an unusual experience, hire a horse and go into the Muskoka Lake section with one of the famous Cowley Fathers, Anglican monks and missionaries. They pack vestments and other liturgical material into saddlebags and ride off to thirty missions in the woods. Hard working always, and silent until noon each day, they have built an imposing church of granite and they teach, farm, sew, and build.

In the Parry Sound Forest District fronting on Georgian Bay (which can be reached by way of Provincial Highway 69), more and more tourists are finding it practical to purchase cottage sites. The attractions, of course, are hunting, fishing, bathing, canoeing, and quiet.

Back to North Bay to continue, briefly, our trip on Route 17, we go to Sudbury, center of a forest land without peer. South from here by Canadian Pacific Railway or Canadian National Railways, or, from Hagar Station by secondary gravel road, lies the French River country. Soon the road from Parry Sound will really open up all this area, but in the meantime, there is plenty of room on the rounded-rock, outcrop shore line of numerous rivers for excellent fishing, and here are more sites which can be bought for campsites. Directly west from Sudbury lie a number of lakes. From Whitefish a secondary gravel road will take you to the unusual Penage Lake, twenty-five miles from Sudbury. Bays and islands, well-wooded shore line of 2,200 miles, lots of deer to be shot, easy accessibility to stores—even a mailbox service at the eastern end of Penage, a real novelty—all these explain why Sudbury will grow as a tourist attraction for years to come. O.S.A. Lake, in the Killarney section along the Georgian Bay has the only known extinct volcano craters in Ontario, which produce panoramas bringing out the artists in their funny hats. (In Sudbury: King Edward, Nickel Range, Frontenac, and Coulson Hotels, and Camp Matagamasine.)

The trip from Sudbury, through Blind River and Thessalon to the "Soo," Route 17, takes you through good lake and hunting country, with occasional glimpses of the North Channel. Sault Ste. Marie environs have just about everything we've credited to other forest areas mentioned, and are strategically located besides. They are reached by excellent highways and by rail through Upper Michigan, by lake boats of both the Canadian Pacific and Canada Steamship Lines, or by a day's drive from Detroit, Chicago, Minneapolis, or Toronto. The "Soo" truly leads to endless tracts of green forests and countless lakes and waterways. Some of the best-known regions are Mississagi, Batchewana, Agawa, and Missinaibi. The area is so large that we can't be too specific, but there are all facilities, from a lean-to in the woods to swanky lodges where even your dog has a cabin. And if you can't catch a fish in this area, hang up your hooks. (At Sault Ste. Marie: Windsor, Grand View, Algoma, and Algonquin Hotels.) Route 17 swings north along the eastern shore of Lake Superior for eighty miles to the Montreal River, with secondary roads leading off to many a summer vacationland. But for a decidedly different trip, where you can see something, and somebody else does all the work, take the Algoma Central Railway north from the "Soo." It leads through Agawa Canyon offering twenty miles of beauty, through forest and towering cliffs and past gleaming lakes. You can go three hundred miles north on this line. (For specific information about this tremendous area, write Department of Lands and Forests, Province of Ontario.)

Now we must return, for the purposes of winding up our already overlong look at this tremendous Neighbor

Worth Knowing, to the North Bay traffic center of Sudbury
for a quick look at the tour north and west, the last one
available to us on good roads, and then, again briefly,
outline a few of the things which can be glimpsed in a
train trip across this vast area. Remember these areas are
comparatively undeveloped and that throughout the trip
almost any place is superb for hunting and fishing. We
can't repeat that in each instance, but it is true. Try to
recall, also, that in making an automobile trip through
these hundreds of miles, you must first check your car
completely, for it is a trip comparable to traversing pre-
war France and Germany combined.

Of Ontario's 412,000 square miles, the great bulk lies
up here in a huge land-and-lake crescent around Lake
Superior. While the thickly populated areas which have
been described are tiny in comparison, they have 60,000
of the province's 80,000 miles of roadway. The key to this
land of nearly two million lakes is the fact that underneath
are the oldest rocks in the world, those of the pre-Cambrian
Shield. For centuries they seemed to symbolize a stony fate
for the area—and then someone stuck a pick in the right
spot and the world could double and treble estimates of
certain mineral reserves. New wealth valued at nearly five
billion dollars has already been discovered, and the Canadians just smile and smile because they know they aren't
half trying, and long after the Americans have given away
everything they've got, there will be time enough to bring
these precious minerals up.

Route 11 north takes you first to Cobalt, where mining
in Ontario got its first real start with the discovery of rich
silver veins. From time to time the mines there run down,
people leave, stores fold up, the future looks tarnished.
Then some bitter-ender stubs his toe on a few thousand
dollars' worth of silver and the panic is on again. (In

Cobalt: the Fraser House.) You go through Englehart past Kirkland's Lake, site of the "Golden Mile" of mines—with gold in 'em, and on to Matheson (Bermont Hotel) where Route 101 turns off to the left to Porcupine, which is simply one gold mine after the other. Timmins is the "same deal" and here is the spot where graduates of renowned universities live in unpainted clapboard houses, raising families, digging gold, having a wonderful time. Inside those rabbit warrens are the latest in radio and record-playing consoles, books, and magazines. These people are modern pioneers, unearthing a brilliant path of gold and silver across the province. The airplane may make prosperous pioneers also out of settlers expected for the great clay belt of Northern Ontario, that area south and west of James Bay, where there are millions of acres of fine farming land that can't be reached. But out of the war came knowledge of how to install cheap and safe airfields and now those fine farming lands may be colonized, supplied, and "marketed" by air transport. (At Timmins: Empire, Timmins, Windsor, and Albert's Hotels.)

A bit farther up the road, but back on Route 11, is Cochrane, jumping-off place for the Temiskaming and Northern Ontario Railway, which, like Route 11, has come from North Bay. In all these towns you may notice the huge shafts rearing ugly heads in the most incongruous places. But up there the shaft goes where the geophysicists say it should go, and no one complains if that happens to be in the front yard or where the bathroom was. (In Cochrane: Albert Hotel and Stevens House.)

Cochrane's depot leads right to an exciting vacation up on James Bay. At Moosonee, the Mounties started their last lap to bring out the infamous Eskimo murderers of Belcher Island, some years ago. And here, on an island, is one of the original Hudson's Bay Posts. Rushing rivers

flow north into the six hundred miles of rolling tidewaters
and there are no roads. In early autumn wild geese rise
above the wastes of James Bay. At the mouth of the Moose
River, on an island, is the ancient settlement of Moose
Factory, which was settled years before the southern part
of the province. The Indians gather here to trade, build
their canoes, and swap news. The oldest blacksmith shop
in Canada is here, and has been in daily use since 1740.

Now back to Cochrane, and we continue our dash over
Route 11, the Trans-Canada road, to Kapuskasing, a model
town (Kapuskasing Inn, Moonlight Camp, and Radio Hotel), and along the Height of Land, where rivers start to
flow north to Hudson Bay. At any spot along here a stout
paddler could leave his car and go by canoe toward the un-
known interior—and adventure. He may be sure that he
will be doing something unique. Now through Hearst
(Palace, Windsor, and Waverley Hotels) through the bush
country to Geraldton, a trip which couldn't have been
made only a few months ago. Completion of this section
of the highway made it possible to travel across the nation
by automobile—possible, but not exactly comfortable yet.
(In Geraldton: Thunder Bay, Geraldton, and Queens
Hotels.)

The road arches alongside mighty Lake Nipigon, which
is seventy miles long, thirty-five miles wide and sprinkled
with more than two thousand islands, going through scenery you'll never match. There are game and fish in incredible abundance. From the waters, deep and clear,
thousand-foot headlands rise unbelievably. There are camps
and resorts too numerous for listing here, but lists of which
can be secured from the provincial publicity people. Thus
we shift from Route 11 to Route 17 and dip down to Port
Arthur and Fort William. This is a great expediting center
on Thunder Bay, head of the Great Lakes, for the grain

of the prairie, the ore, and the pulp and paper which must
be moved everywhere by boat and rail. The town is laid
out on a huge scale, with long streets, big squares, and few
houses but many monoliths of grain elevators dominating
everything. At night certain sections of it look as empty as
you'd imagine a city up here might if blown up by an
atomic bomb. (Prince Arthur, Mariaggi, and New Ontario
Hotels in Port Arthur; Royal Edward, Alexandra, and
Adanac Hotels in Fort William.)

As a visitor to the lakehead you'll be shown beautiful
Kakabeka Falls, the Sleeping Giant, a spectacular coffin
mountain, Loch Lomond, and, perhaps, Pigeon River. All
around you are the vistas of tomorrow, big things in the
doing. The Canadian Pacific running through the town
curls out around the edge of Lake Superior on what will
someday likely be one of the scenic trips of the world,
when the highway is completed beyond Schreiber, and on
down to Marathon, which represents the transformation of
a wicked frontier camp to a rich, respectable, modern
town, built on order. There's a fifteen-million-dollar pulp
mill, a new hospital with the latest from pills to penicillin,
and housing with rentals based on 43 per cent of value.
The United States could learn a few tricks examining the
race Marathon has run thus far!

But getting back to Port Arthur and Fort William, double doorways to the West, we take Route 17 up through
more lakes, past the land of a thousand lakes, among
the towering white pines in the "forest primeval," in an
air-conditioned climate which averages 60 degrees, and
thus on up to the Lake-of-the-Woods section, first passing
through Dryden (Central and Dryden Hotels, Rutter's
Cabins). For many years my Minnesota friends have been
telling me how they either take a boat from Beaudette,
on their end of the Lake of the Woods, to Kenora, or

drive on Route 71 until they hit Canadian Route 70, thence north to either Sioux Narrows or Reed Narrows, for fine fishing. There are dozens of resorts along the routes, and forty-five miles farther on is Kenora, at one end of the lake and encircled by smaller lakes. (Camp Canuck, Shelton's Canadian Camps, and others average $6.00 a day, American plan.) After you "fish out" Kenora you can take Route 17 east, and then north, to Lake Vermilion, a great spot for muskies. (Vermilion Bay Lodge, Bayview Hotel, or Bratland's Camp.) Minnesotans tell me they drove the 115 miles north to Red Lake Town and fished in Red Lake, then had to return over the same route, because that was the end of the line. Back on Route 17 they went east again for a few miles, then turned left to Sioux Lookout, which is another blind alley from which you must retrace your miles, but worth it if you are a fisherman or a "scenery man." These people always drove back down Route 17 to Upsala (Upsala Inn) and to Kennebeck Falls, which, though hard to get to, are 129 feet high and very beautiful. Then they drove back to Port Arthur, turned northeast to Lake Neopengion, miles and miles of traveling among idyllic trees and rocks, then back to the States at Pigeon River, after seeing the Pigeon River Falls. They always make it sound like the best thing that ever happened to them.

A train trip through Northern Ontario isn't as tiring as a motor trip, but then it isn't as rewarding, either. My trip was made exceedingly interesting through a chance meeting with John Fisher, the eminent Canadian Broadcasting Company radio reporter. Everywhere I had gone, in the Maritimes, Montreal, Quebec, Toronto, people who had desired to give me information had said: "John Fisher knows all about that; yes, look up John Fisher." So, one morning as the train was steaming along through interminable forests and by the edges of interminable streams, I went to the dining car and sat down—and there was John Fisher! From then on I took more of an interest, and many more notes. He populated the gleaming streams with *voyageurs,* pointed out the battleground of the Crees and Iroquois at Kukatush, and at Foleyet guided me down to the baggage car, so that we saw the unloading of canoes and supplies for several parties striking out for the bush. At Peterbell, John said: "We now come upon the Missinaibi, which for many years was the route of the fur brigades to James Bay." At Shekak he said, "Here's the river called 'Shekak,' which means 'skunk,' but the name is definitely off-scent for such a wonderful trout stream."

At Longlac, head of a finger lake fifty-five miles long, we saw an interesting crowd down to order their supplies for gold mining, like farmers going through the Sears, Roebuck catalog at home. At Armstrong we put our watches back an hour, which somehow seemed excuse for a little ceremony. John's secretary produced paper cups for said formality. We stayed up to see Sioux Lookout and meet a friend of John's, a Catholic priest who was going to fly into the northland the next morning. This vicinity is good not only for hunting and fishing but copper, gold, silver, and fine grades of white marble and black granite. In the early morning the train stopped at Minaki, a popular summer resort on island-dotted reaches of the Winnipeg River, main waterway for a basin of 55,000 square miles and producer of 300,000 horsepower of electric current annually.

Malaki, at the northern end of the lake by the same name, was reached, and then we knew we were leaving Ontario's ever interesting scenery for the sameness of the prairie. At Ophir, a tiny station, John Fisher said, "You are now in Manitoba, beyond the rim of adventure."

· II ·

Manitoba

THERE IS only one paved road leading into Manitoba and the Keystone province is truly labeled "beyond the rim of adventure."

In a very real sense, Manitoba was founded by "The Governor and Company of Adventurers of England trading into Hudson Bay"—the Hudson's Bay Company. This select group of retailers fought wars, made treaties, gave out letters of patent, flew their own flag (and still do, even though Canada hasn't one!) and had complete sway as "true and absolute Lordes and Proprietors," over a land so large that you could have lost the domain of the original grantor (England) in the remotest, teeny corner of it. Their charter included the provinces of Quebec and Ontario (north of the Laurentians and west of Labrador), Manitoba, Saskatchewan, the southern half of Alberta, the southeast corner of the North West Territories, most of British Columbia, and the American states of Washington and Oregon. Today "The Bay" operates a chain of fine department stores noted for excellent blankets, whisky, rum, and other products, and a museum of unexcelled Canadiana which you must visit when you go to Winnipeg. It has set the pace in Manitoba, which is still the spot for an adventurer.

Manitoba is about the size of France, or of the states of Minnesota, Wisconsin, Illinois, and Iowa combined. It is usually referred to as a prairie province, when actually 75 per cent of it is wooded. And it has its Vassar, Dallas,

Brokenhead, Reykjavik, Magnet, and Garson, but not Greer. They're all small towns, and the Bloodvein is a river.

The people are friendly and, on the whole, cheerful. They are of all bloods known to man, but the majority of them are Nordic types, with here and there a cluster of Bessarabian blood around the onion-bulb churches, which seems fitting, for this is the start of Canada's "Ukraine." These people travel much, and this is reflected in a better vacation time for you, since they are inclined to be more receptive and friendly, almost like the breezy Westerners.

For motorists the main point of entry into Manitoba is at Emerson, where Provincial Trunk Highway Number 14 joins with U.S. Highways 81 and 75. Another, increasingly popular, gateway takes you through the lovely and meaningful International Peace Gardens, as U.S. Highway 3 joins Manitoba's scenic Highway Number 10, which is the direct avenue to Riding Mountain National Park and the romance which lies, as Manitobans put it, "north of 53" which means beyond 53 degrees of latitude.

Manitoba can be reached by Greyhound Bus, which line has frequent service from United States points to Winnipeg. And from the capital, buses run to all Manitoba points, with a twice-a-day schedule to all near-by beaches and resorts in the summertime.

Seventy-five trains arrive and depart daily at Winnipeg railway stations. Five trains each day are transcontinental, east and west, making Montreal in thirty-five hours and Vancouver in forty-eight. Northern Pacific, Great Northern, and Soo Line operate trains each day to Minneapolis, while to Duluth there is a six-times-a-week service. Both of Canada's great rail lines have week-end excursions from Winnipeg to the resort areas on Lake Winnipeg, while The Pas and Flin Flon get six trains a week. From there the Hudson Bay Railroad will huff you and puff you up to Churchill upon your selection from their twice-weekly schedule.

By air, Fargo, North Dakota, and Minneapolis are connected with Winnipeg by two daily flights by Northwest Airlines. Trans-Canada operates four transcontinental flights daily, both east and west, from Winnipeg, and Canadian Pacific has regularly scheduled flights between Winnipeg, Dauphin, The Pas, and Flin Flon. You may charter flights to almost anywhere in the north country, and there are regular flights up to Churchill. The rules previously outlined for you if you fly in in your own plane hold true, again, in Manitoba. After proper notification, fly in to any field where you may be inspected.

Entering Canada on Highway 14, the only paved entranceway linking up with pavement on the other side of the border, it is only an easy couple of hours' drive (sixty miles) to Winnipeg. But there is always something to be gained in a leisurely trip. Next the customhouse in Emerson is a provincial travel information booth, for detailed information. Twelve miles north and you arrive at Letellier, famous meeting ground of Indian hunters, and burial place of the first white man to die in Manitoba. There's a cairn over his grave. Nine miles more and you've made it to St. Jean, where there's good French cooking done by people who are descendants of the first settlers to trade a ten-cent geegaw for a ten-dollar fur. They have square dances, come Saturday night, and French she is *populaire.* Then comes Morris, which is as easy to take as the chair by the same name, and later, Ste. Agathe, with its large church, convent, shaded Red River, interesting side roads and farmers—their nation's backbone—with whom to talk. At St. Norbert the men in your party are allowed to visit monks at the Monastery of Our Lady of the Prairies. No women are allowed into the sanctuary of these hooded men of an order more than a thousand years old. Trappist cheese may be purchased beyond the elaborate iron-grill gates.

After Ste. Agathe you are almost in the suburbs of Winnipeg, capital of the province. Mix the Red River with the Assiniboine River and you get "dirty waters," which is the translation of the name "Winnipeg." The capital has over 200,000 population, with another 100,000 or so hanging onto its urban apron strings. This makes it by far the largest city in the prairies. The streets seem overwide and clean, the buildings pleasing, the homes, especially those of the old cereal tycoons, imposing and interesting in a rococo fashion.

The people are friendly, cheerful, and of such an exuberance that the city was the birthplace of the Red River reel, terpsichorean test for heart, limbs, lungs, and endurance, involving intricacies of the Highland fling, the Irish jig, and something of an Indian war dance. (The Honorable James Mackay, 320 pounds, was light of foot in the Red River reel, "like a bubble in a breeze.") Winnipeg also has the world's largest "bonspiel," the second largest grain market, and one of the most important fur markets. In the lobby of the Fort Garry Hotel I overheard two Americans, both apparently from the Deep South, quizzing an assistant manager about curling.

"Take the name," said one. " 'Bon' means good, and 'spiel,' I take it, means talk. 'A good talk fest,' eh?"

"Well, no sir," replied the assistant manager. "You see they throw rocks—"

"Throw rocks!" broke in the second Southerner. "Good heavens, I thought Canadians were gent—"

"Well you see," said the hotel man in some confusion, "the rules are that these rocks have to be the same, forty pounds, and with iron handles in them, and they're not exactly throwing them *at* each other; they're *curling* with them."

"Curling, eh. Some curls you could get with rocks weighing forty pounds," was the somewhat doubting reply. "Let's begin all over, suh."

So they began all over and it seemed a bit difficult for the comprehension of the men from Georgia, or Louisiana, or Florida. But curling is increasingly popular, both in Canada and the northern states of the United States bordering on it. Every town has its curling team and rink and now the great national contests for both men and women are like our world series in baseball. Each community had its sports day, too, generally in the summer, for baseball, softball, swimming, and horse racing. In the winter there are curling, figure skating, dog-team racing, and all the sports of an ice carnival.

The best "show" in Winnipeg, in my opinion, is to be found in the museum on the fourth floor of the Hudson's Bay Company store. It tells you pictorially the history of the "Bay" and of Manitoba, which, as has been related, are practically synonymous. With careful study you can see how the "Bay" dwindled from a sovereign body to just another department store. The store, once a trading post, was located strategically at the confluence of the rivers, and as was expected, Fort Garry was near by. The gate of the old fort is all that is left today, because townspeople used the remaining stone for foundations for their homes. Winnipeg began in that general vicinity of the railroad station, the "Bay," and Fort Garry, and today, with the imposing Parliament Building and two of the finest public or semipublic parks I have ever seen anywhere, represents the principal point of interest, from a tourist standpoint.

Bruce Boreham, another of the Canadian National Railways' excellent public-relations men, had just gotten back to Winnipeg from Jasper National Park, where Bing Crosby had won the golf tournament, a turn of events calculated to win kudos for any press agent. Mr. Boreham drove through the tree-lined avenues, showing me the fine private gardens which make of the city a thing of beauty. Every street seems as wide as the Champs Elysées, but with shade everywhere.

"Over there across the river," said Bruce, "is St. Boniface, a corner of French culture known to millions through Whittier's famous lines:

" 'The Bells of the Roman Mission
          That call from the turrets twain,
   To the boatman on the river
          To the hunter on the plain. . . .'

"They'll be ringing the Angelus again this evening as they have called the faithful for over a century."

As we passed the building where they hold the fur auctions I laughingly recalled John Fisher's excellent script about it, *Million-Dollar Skin Game*. The auctioneer faces a group of silent men sitting in folding chairs and sells thousands of dollars' worth of furs, although none is in sight and the casual observer could never detect any of the buyers in their bidding. They've seen the furs upstairs, marked their catalogs, and since they don't want the others to know what they are buying, have secret signs which they relay to flunkies, called spotters, on the side lines. A raised eyebrow, a flip of a pencil, a hand placed on the back of the head and the bid is made and bellowed out to the auctioneer. For here, from the beginning of Manitoba, men have dealt in furs to warm and win the hearts of the women of the world.

"It was Sadie Hawkins Day in reverse in early Winnipeg," Bruce said. "From the very first there were a thousand men to every five hundred women. Any personable chick arriving in Winnipeg could count on less than three days of spinsterhood. Now the situation is normal and the gals buy tons of perfumes, deodorants, and beauty aids just like your girls at home. But back there they only had two questions: Did she have leprosy; and first, would she marry?"

We drove around the miles and miles of parks, saw the great half-timbered pavilion in Assiniboine Park, and the buffalo, fittingly kept in splendor, the faunal emblem of Manitoba. Since Bruce was a railroad man, but from another line, I went along to see the Countess of Dufferin, ancient bell-funneled locomotive, first to reach rails for prairie service. It was brought on a barge from the United States, via the Red River, and with steam up ran ashore onto tracks previously laid for it, with a Western welcome of bells, whistles, bands, and gunfire drowning out the clamor of its own exertions. It got its name because Lady Dufferin, later the Countess, was on hand. For ten years it did the whistle stops near-by while the Canadian Pacific Railway lines crawled slowly toward Winnipeg and then, in 1886, joined the big leagues of railroading.

Hotel accommodation in Winnipeg has come a long way since the day when George Emmerley started the first hostel with a total initial capital of a barrel of whisky and two barrels of apples. (No, I don't know what he wanted with all those apples.) The Canadian National Railways has the excellent Fort Garry, the Canadian Pacific Railway the very fine Royal Alexandra, and there are the Marlborough, the St. Charles, and several other fine hotels, and the Granite and Riverwood Cabins. There are good restaurants at the hotels named, and the Hudson Bay Dining Room, Childs, Moore's, and the Blackstone. I also enjoyed the Chocolate Shop. Sometimes in Manitoba you can get the excellent, thick pea soup which, as I should have mentioned, is also obtainable in Quebec, and Pioneer pie, made of a ragout of game, as well as excellent homemade berry pies.

From all that thinking about food we turn to some food for thought. Winnipeg is in a very favored location, in the center of the continent, and it is Manitoba's natural road center. So we'll use Winnipeg as our center peg and radiate out on trips to cover the province, or that part of it which is paved, or as good as paved, and also that section which you reach by rail.

Route 1, leading east from Winnipeg a short distance to the Ontario line, is of course, the road we would take if we could pursue these trips in the logical fashion, that is from east to west across the continent. But since the Ontario highway connecting up isn't paved, we'll reverse the process so as to visit the great Whiteshell Forest Reserve, land of antiquity, where yesterday meets today, where North shakes hands with South. From the United States border over Route 14, then changing to Route 1, you can drive to the Whiteshell in an easy day's tour. At Garson the Trans-Canada road runs right through the quarries whence is carved the exquisite Tyndall marble. Beausejour means "Pleasant Stay," no misnomer at the Beausejour and Howland Hotels.

Farther on, Route 11 branches off for the Lac du Bonnet-Pine Falls area, known as the Wonderland of Eastern Manitoba, myriads of evergreen trees lining the shores of countless lakes, the Winnipeg River roaring, as at Silver Falls, or serene in typically Pre-Cambrian country. Route 11 is an all-weather gravel road.

However if the Whiteshell is your destination, continue

along Route 1 to Whitemouth, one of the province's oldest and quietest settlements, and go on to Rennie, eighteen miles farther on and located just at the edge of the park. The Whiteshell is a thousand square miles of forests, lakes, and river, an evergreen playground of more than two hundred lakes. Although traversed by La Verendrye, one of the earliest of travelers through Manitoba, in 1734, its beauties lay virtually undiscovered until the Trans-Canada Highway was opened in 1932. Cold granite cliffs rise out of sparkling lakes; there are open glades perfect for picnic grounds. Here can be seen Ojibway ceremonial mosaics—best preserved neolithic art on the continent—and here savages danced to wild tom-toms and said it with stone billboards to their gods. All this, and superb canoeing and fishing for pickerel (walleyes), northern pike, perch, bass, and lake trout; hunting is allowed in part of the park.

It is legal to stalk and kill on the north side of the Canadian National Railways' tracks through the park, but not on the south side. Of the many lodges and cabins, Lake Brereton Lodge, Jessica Lake Bungalow Camp, White Lake Bungalow Camp, and Manahan's Bear Lake Camp are recommended.

A most enjoyable jaunt north from Winnipeg is a six-day cruise on the S.S. *Keenora* into Lake Winnipeg, ninth largest lake in the world. Leaving Monday morning you are back Saturday afternoon, having been more than three hundred miles into the northland, past the magic line of "53," and have glided to many a landing at tiny lakeside Indian villages which your memory will hold forever. The *Keenora* is a sturdy steel vessel with sleeping accommodations for a hundred. She has an Indian crew, and on her deck will be as queer an assortment of passengers as ever signed the list. Mounties "going in" after a vacation in Winnipeg, teachers for Indian schools, sourdoughs, bush pilots, sometimes even those romantic King's Messengers, bound for nobody knows where.

"For the first few hours," says John Fisher, whose stories on Manitoba have interested scores of thousands, "the *Keenora* sails down the Red River from the place you board her, which is at a large floating dock back of a brewery. On one side of the narrow Red you can see the square white Scotch and English farms, and villages with spired churches and names like St. Andrews and Selkirk. On the other bank, just as though it were a different country, are the Ukrainian and Balkan settlements. Their farmhouses are gay, painted in bright pinks and yellows with bright blue roofs. They look like chalets out of a Walt Disney movie."

After the locks, John continues, comes Lake Winnipeg, so large it is like the ocean, and with points along its shores to visit in the heart of the trapper and trader country: Famous Hudson's Bay trading posts where you can buy needlework and souvenirs, where you'll see planes take off for the north or where the boat will nose into a cove to bring aboard a sick trapper. And 'way up there on the north end is Norway House, outpost of the Hudson's Bay Company. You may stay over if you choose. There's a first-class inn, with tennis, canoeing, and hiking to be enjoyed when the spirit moves you.

A port of call on some Lake Winnipeg sailings is Gimli, largest Icelandic town in Canada. If you visit there in August you'll see Icelandic native costumes and hear ancient folk songs as the national holiday of Iceland is celebrated. Gimli in Icelandic mythology was the residence of Odin, where all good and brave men went after death. Incidentally, Reykjavik is over on Lake Manitoba.

The other main highway into Manitoba is Number 10, which begins in the International Peace Gardens of the

Turtle Mountain Forest Reserve. "To God in His Glory," reads the inscription on a tablet in a cairn, "we two nations dedicate this garden, and pledge ourselves that as long as men shall live, we will not take up arms against one another." The first town of any size is Boissevain, where hundreds set out each year for the Killarney Lake area to the east. But off to the left is another favorite tourist point, the Souris Valley. In the marshlands over there is the small town of Pierson, where the professional dog trainers gather each summer and put their pets through "college" courses in pointing and retrieving. No doubt the degrees are all Cum Lassie.

Brandon, second largest town in Manitoba, is next. (Places to stay are: Prince Edward, Cecil, Brondon, Beaulier, Grandview, and Wheat City Hotels.) This is the Wheat City, where farmers come to annual fairs to buy heavy machinery and pink cotton candy. Off to the right there, Route 1 stretches through Carberry and Portage la Prairie to Winnipeg, the longest bit of paved road in the province. But north lies much of interest. Follow Route 10 to Riding Mountain National Park, the highest area in Manitoba, rolling hill country averaging 2,200 feet above sea level. There are the typical attractions of such a park, and some very fine accommodations (the Chalet, Pioneer Hotel, Ta-Wa-Pit Lodge, Wasagaming Lodge, and Bungalows and Idylwylde [where do they get those names?] Bungalows).

Off to the left of its southern rim, on Route 4 is the little town of Birtle, home of my friends, the C. Leroy Duttons. Mr. Dutton, former mayor of the town and once its druggist, is an inveterate curler and sports fan, as is his charming wife. One would expect very little recreation in a town of six hundred souls, but the citizens of Birtle have tied a stemming knot in Bird Tail Creek, forming a lake where in summer they dunk themselves, and their broods are taught swimming by experts who have made the five-hour drive from Winnipeg. Winters provide them with plain ice skating and fancy figure skating, and they go curling as far away as Toronto, maybe. In fall they hunt ducks. Sports Day is Dominion Day, July 1, and everybody is out to the baseball game and other events. On the edge of the lake are cabins and cottages which rent for from $10 to $15 a week during summer seasons.

Thus north to Dauphin, an up-and-coming town in the middle of lush farmlands, where Route 10 swings left to Ashville and then north, close to the line of Duck Mountain Forest Reserve. Singoosh Lake in the Forest Reserve is a happy place to fish and leave canoe tracks. Swan River has a good tourist camp, exceptional scenery, and fighting fish. Another 150 miles through undeveloped country and skirting the edge of Dawson Bay brings you to The Pas, the fabled town where cautious motorists think of turning back, and the truly adventurous make plans to go to Flin Flon or even white-whale hunting up at Churchill. The Pas is a gateway to the Arctic. Its newspaper editor operates what he calls the "Moccasin Telegraph." It is merely a wooden pew alongside his desk where people of the north sit and tell him what they know when they reach town. They know just about everything going on—for up there white men are conspicuous. Perhaps the word is that a party of hunters from Detroit was seen "going in." Or they'll tell of the progress of the muskrat trapping in the Summerberry, where the government, having restored the breeding grounds by artificially flooding the marshes, allocated a certain number of rats to each hunter, and where in the winter whole families with all their belongings go in on caterpillar trains, huge tractors hauling big sleds over the ice. Or maybe huge herds of caribou have stalled the Iceberg Special, the train to Churchill. Beavers could do it, too. They sometimes move into culverts and dam them up, inundating the roadbed. When such things happen a little man jumps on a railway handcar and pumps like mad to the scene, traps Mr. Beaver in a bailey net and takes him to a new scene of operations where he can get his mind off culverts.

The Pas has a famed old Anglican church with hand-hewn pews and tablets, so help me, in the Cree Indian language. The train from there takes you through wild country with only a stop or two—unless someone requests it. Once, not so very long ago, a pretty woman asked the conductor to stop at Mile 66. He did, and she stepped off and walked to Lake Athapapuskow, which is a lake such as you should fish in once and then call all fishing that follows anticlimactic. This young lady, Miss Leone Hayes, then trolled for a time and landed a lake trout weighing sixty-three pounds and measuring forty-seven and one-half inches!—perhaps the longest and biggest lake trout ever caught. It is stuffed and now dominates the wall at the Game and Fisheries Office of the Provincial Legislature Building at Winnipeg. That's the story of Mile 66, and the Lady and the Monster.

In Flin Flon you'll find a modern city built around some of the world's largest copper mines. There are taxis and private cars, but other than the city streets they haven't anywhere to go; yes, and sidewalks up in the air so far that they need, and have, handrails. They're built on the city sewers, which, because of the solid rock thereabouts, couldn't be buried except at tremendous cost. You walk down to go into a store. Electric power is so cheap that at Island Falls, near by, everyone uses it for heating, and there were, until a year or so ago, only a couple of chimneys in the place. They keep the lights on all day up there so the filament inside the bulbs won't be destroyed by the cold and the change in temperature. Up in Churchill, the only ocean port for the prairie land, great grain elevators ring the harbor. Many an American can tell you how the white whales, some of them weighing two thousand pounds, throw their blubber about the bay. They are hunted by men in power-driven small boats, who first harpoon, then shoot them. It is a thrilling and dangerous sport, and Canadian National Railways runs special trains up there packed to the sills with hunters when white whale are running.

The United States installation at Churchill will probably be of some interest to Americans, and not far from these ultramodern works are the ruins of Fort Prince of Wales which was built by the British and then fell to the French. The rusted guns are in place and there is a stone which reads "S¹ Hearne, July ye 1. 1767." Sammy Hearne was the gent who found the Coppermine River and traced it all the way to the Arctic Sea, first white man to do it. That's why the stone is interesting; for there's many an old tombstone with older date. Churchill may have a future as a grain port or as a battleground. It depends upon whether the world plumps for peace or suicide. Here in Churchill they know more than they can reveal about substances which are essential for the making of atomic bombs.

Now for a quick trip across Manitoba by train, and then we'll turn toward Saskatchewan. Although the land seems level, you gain eighty-six feet of altitude in going from Winnipeg to Portage la Prairie. Portage is the trading center for a highly successful farm area which is watered by the Assiniboine River. When the western lands were parched for years on end, Portage's hinterland raised record-breaking crops. Here they developed the wheat varieties which made Canada famous.

Rivers is the first divisional railway point west of Winnipeg, which is great stuff to railroad people and doesn't mean a damned thing to others. Miniota was named by the Assiniboin Indians, or Stony Indians, who gave that sort of reception to the settlers hereabouts. At Lazare, it's merely across the Qu'Appelle River Valley to the ruins of Fort Ellice, a Hudson's Bay Post of earliest times, but I didn't get off the train to see it. At Victor the train crosses from Manitoba to Saskatchewan, and we end on a Victorious note.

· 12 ·

The World of Wheat

N<small>O, THERE</small>'s nothing in Saskatoon that I could recommend that a tourist should see," said the lady in the Tourist Bureau office in this, Saskatchewan's second largest city. "And in the province as a whole there's nothing but the parks. No, you'd have to have a hunting or fishing place in mind, recommended by some friend, and go directly to that, in order to want to come to Saskatchewan. No, there aren't any paved roads in the province, except just a few miles around one or two of the principal cities. Tourists call us on the phone, call to the nearest tourist office, ask about the condition of the roads, and we tell them. In most cases if it has rained they can't drive over the roads."

I examined the printed form prepared by the Saskatchewan Motor Club and Tourist Bureau, describing each numbered route as to paving, miles graveled, and miles otherwise worked on, with a space to write in its daily condition. Then I picked up that very day's issue of the *Saskatoon Star-Phoenix*. On the front page there was an article headed: N<small>O</small> G<small>RAVEL ON</small> P<small>RINCE</small> A<small>LBERT</small> H<small>IGHWAY</small>; R<small>AIN</small> M<small>AKES</small> D<small>RIVING</small> T<small>ERRIBLE</small>. The reporter described how this route to the province's number one tourist attraction, Prince Albert National Park, was "absolutely shocking," and how his car got stuck in the mud, there being "precious little gravel."

"To call the Saskatoon–Prince Albert road a graveled highway is not only inaccurate but absolutely false and misleading," he wrote. "It took a tractor to move the car on the road. It was not in the ditch, or in difficulty. The only trouble was it was on the road, which was quite passable twenty-five years ago, but impossible now. It appears that the municipalities and the provincial government are still carrying on an argument as to which authority should be responsible for ferry approaches. Four truck loads of gravel would fix the road, yet Saskatchewan continues to bleat for more tourist traffic. It will never come with such bad roads, and if tourists do their visiting in Saskatchewan they'll never return after seeing such a mess as provincial highway Number 12 was after a few hours' rain on Saturday."

Another story under an Ottawa date line told how the total tourist trade in Canada was officially estimated as passing the quarter-billion-dollar mark spent by twenty-five million visitors, a big increase, but that Saskatchewan, of all the provinces, showed a decrease in the number of visiting cars.

After a thorough check I found that the lady in the tourist information office was partially correct; but only partially. There are reasons why American tourists should want to visit her province. But the reporter was accurate. Some of the roads are atrocious. And I learned that the province of Saskatchewan is already getting as many tourists as it has any right to, considering the present state of its roads and accommodations.

Saskatchewan is Canada's leading agricultural province. The world knows it for the production of wheat, largely thinks of it as a flat, monotonous roll and ripple of cereals dotted here and there over the miles by men working on machines or behind horses, and by occasional farmhouses, frequently unpainted and almost always with milk cans on a collection rack in front of the house and a Chic Sale special behind it. There is, however, a timbered, watered, green, and attractive "half" of the province, the upper section. It is not as spectacular or interesting as in other provinces, and again, there are the roads, or lack of them, to hamper tourists in getting to this section.

By far the best road in the province is Route 1, the Trans-Canada Highway, from the Manitoba border through Regina and Moose Jaw to Alberta. It is 462 miles in length, of which 116 are hard surfaced. This route enters the province at Fleming and parallels the course of the Canadian Pacific Railway to Indian Head, which in the early days of wheat farming was the center of a single farm of a hundred square miles. Furrows four miles long were the custom on that farm, and since nothing was mechanized in those days, it took a ploughman half a day to plough a furrow out and the other half a day for him to trace another one back, just in time to keep from starving to death, if you know farm hands. From Indian Head a fourteen-mile side trip over Route 56 will take you to the first tourist attraction, Katepwe Provincial Park, situated on one of four long and narrow lakes in the flat country. Carefully tended beaches are the main attraction, although there is also golf, boating, and fishing. Rates for rooms are reasonable at the Katepwe Lodge, part of the famous Qu'Appelle Valley resorts.

Qu'Appelle, next to the west from Indian Head, is a musical name recalling the adventurous days of the Hudson's Bay Company fur trappers and traders. Twenty miles north of the town there is an Old Post on the Fishing Lakes, Fort Qu'Appelle, on the river by the same name. From a rock face over one of these quiet pools there's an echo which has been famous for about a century. This is the origin of the name, "Qu'Appelle," or in English, "Who calls?"

It is only an hour-and-a-half's drive from this town to Regina, capital of the province. Besides the government offices and the interesting Crown corporations, an attempt on the part of the government to go into business for the people, this is the center of the powerful people's lobbies on their own behalf, through co-operatives. As the Bread Basket of Empire, Saskatchewan is too much dependent upon one crop and the vagaries of world politics concerning that single crop: wheat. If it isn't the weather, then it's the rat's nest of world politics. Thus, the harassed plains farmer is the ward of his own government and the pawn of all governments.

Regina is a fairly pretty city, with shade and public parks, an outstanding hotel, the Hotel Saskatchewan, and a fine-looking Legislative Building set in 167 acres of trees and flowers. It also has a legitimate tourist attraction, the Royal Canadian Mounted Police exhibits. A lot of froth has been written about these cops on horseback, much of which they resent. A little discernment on your part will reveal they are still cops, as reporters from all over the world learned when they covered the 1939 visit of the King and Queen of England to Canada.

A short trip north (Route 11) to Lumsden puts you within range of forty-mile-long Last Mountain Lake, with its innumerable beaches. Back on Route 1 the road is fine to Moose Jaw, like Regina a wholesale distribution center, also a divisional point of the Canadian Pacific Railway. A small boy solemnly assured me that the town got its name because "this is where Samson mended the covered wagon with the jawbone of a mule." He was as mixed up as a contestant on a quiz show, but Moose Jaw is popularly supposed to have been so named because a white man fixed his wagon with the jawbone of a moose. (Others say it comes from the manner in which the place is laid out.)

Moose Jaw has about 21,000 inhabitants, and a high percentage of them must play billiards and pool, according to the street signs. It has the excellent Grant Hall Hotel and several others, some parks, and a natatorium which would do credit to many cities much larger.

After leaving this thriving community, another short drive brings you to Swift Current, population 5,000, and then comes Gull Lake, followed by Maple Creek, which is where Sitting Bull, the Sioux Indian chief, was captured by a Mountie, following the massacre of General Custer and his men at the Little Big Horn.

A short dip south, over a questionable road, brings you to Cypress Hills Provincial Park, set amidst pine, spruce, and aspen. A lodge has been provided, as well as additional cabins. It is only sixty-three miles from Maple Creek to Medicine Hat, Alberta. In tracing Route 1 across the province we have followed the tracks of the Canadian Pacific Railway.

The best routes from the United States are Number 6, which connects up with Montana's 16 and 13 and then goes straight north to Regina; or Saskatchewan's 39, which connects up with a number of roads in North Dakota and also runs through Regina. Or North Dakota's 52 and 8 link up with Saskatchewan's Route 9, and bring you to Moose Mountain Provincial Park where a handsome stone-faced chalet faces Lake Kenosee, in the center of an area of game, boating, and fishing.

Any of these routes will take you to Saskatoon, the province's second city, but perhaps Route 39 to Moose Jaw and Route 2 and 11 through Craik and Hanley are best. Saskatoon was named for a berry, by prohibitionists, and now lives, in part, on oats. Quaker Oats has a plant here, as has Robin Hood Flour. The city has come a long way in a couple of generations. Around 1881 a group of people who couldn't stand the drinking and helling around in Toronto, organized the Temperance Colonization Society, and moved out to the plains. Also there was the Barr Colony, which came from England under the Reverend Isaac Barr and settled about two hundred miles farther west, became dissatisfied, and came back to Saskatoon. These early people used to buy reddish-purple berries from the Indians, who called them saskatoons. Thus the place got its start and its name.

Pies made from these berries are famous. You can get them fresh in the early fall or made from the canned fruit any time. The early temperance influence lingers on, too. Now the daily legal allowance for one person is: one quart of liquor, one gallon of wine, and twenty-four pints of beer. If you want any more than that you have to go to a public house, where you can be served only beer.

At the excellent Hotel Bessborough in Saskatoon I met many excellent citizens of this progressive city. They told me stories about the Mounties, brought two or three retired detectives over for me to talk to, and told me about the Bentley boys, who played first-rate hockey. Douglas and Max Bentley were two great stars of the Chicago Blackhawks, and the hockey influence was so great around their home that one of the girls became a star, and they made up a family team. Eric Knowles, managing editor of the *Star-Phoenix*, which has a circulation of 30,000 and better in a city of 50,000, told me about the people building a community hockey and curling rink through popular subscription, and how they have supported a fifty-piece symphony orchestra for years. He also told me about Gus Kenderdine, who recently died at seventy-six after having led a colony of true Saskatchewan artists. Gus was going through the city on his way to Japan, liked the place, and never left it. He taught art at the University of Saskatche-

wan. Some of his paintings hang at the Nutana Collegiate
Institute in the city.

General talk concerned the return of deer, now present
by the thousands, and of the pronghorn antelope, which
may be seen within a hundred miles of the city. Businessmen fly to the north and hunt caribou in arctic wastes. Lac
la Ronge, not that far, yet getting up there into the vast-
ness of pre-Cambrian rocks, wild rivers, and muskeg, has
2,000 islands. A road has been built up there, an extension
of Highway Number 2, through Prince Albert, Prince
Albert National Park, and on to the new town of La
Ronge, on the edge of the great lake. For an adventurer
this is a great trip, they tell me. You have come over a
white ribbon running through the dark green of forests,
around the rims of hundreds of unnamed lakes, a hundred
miles past the previous limits of habitations, into the land
of the Indian, Metis, and white hunters, trappers, and
fishermen. These cold waters are the province's best fishing grounds. Cabins are being built, but you'd better bring
your own tents and blankets.

Another highway is being laid down from White Fox,
northeast of Prince Albert, to Flin Flon, Manitoba, 140
miles to the northeast. It will open up some of the finest
sporting country in Canada.

Prince Albert, gateway city to the north, can be reached
on Route 2, which runs right up through the center of the
province, as previously noted, or over the road where the
reporter's car got stuck, Route 12 through Duck Lake, 108
miles north of Saskatoon. Prince Albert has a population
of almost 13,000, and is the province's fourth city. From
here it is thirty-six miles (over Route 2, also) to the corner
of the park, and another thirty-three miles to headquarters
at Waskesiu. There is a small town with its garages, beau-
ticians, laundries, and drugstores, and seven places to stay,

including Lakeview Hotel, Pleasant Inn, Red Deer Chalet, Waskesiu Lodge, Spruce Lodge, and Hillcrest and Waskesiu Bungalows. In the summertime there is far better than average canoeing (scores of lakes and streams link up), swimming in hundreds of fine lakes at an invigorating altitude, and the usual hiking and photographing old Hudson's Bay forts and trail crossings. In the wintertime Prince Albert plays host at an annual ski tournament.

Both Canadian National Railways and Canadian Pacific Railway run very comprehensive mileage all over the province. Until the roads materialize, perhaps it would be better to decide where you want to go in Saskatchewan and then weigh very carefully the possibility of going there by train. I've always found train travel very comfortable. Let's hope that one of these days Saskatchewan will overcome her financial difficulties and build more and better roads. But in the meantime let's give her credit for what she has done; her area is greater than that of any nation in Europe, twice as large as the British Isles, as large as France, Belgium, and Holland combined, and yet she has less than a million people, with a large percentage of the heads of farm families heavily in debt and only wishing they could pay taxes.

Even today, if you've got a jeep and a strong stomach; if you don't mind dust and bumps and primitive wildness without many conveniences or very many things well organized for you to do (except hunting, swimming, canoeing, and fishing), Saskatchewan will serve, and you'll get a friendly welcome.

· 13 ·

Incomparable Alberta

P ART OF the standard of living of America is the wilds of Canada," writes Gregory Clark, a newspaperman friend of mine. He must have been thinking of Alberta. "Canada is fortunate," he writes, "in having considerable areas forever unfit for anything save recreation."

We can hope the reporter is accurate in his prediction; however in the bulges of pre-Cambrian rock, mountain chains, and masses of river-laced muskeg there already have been found radioactive substances, especially uranium, and metals essential to World War III. There is no telling where the materials for World War XX are going to be discovered, and my bet is that if these "necessary" materials turn up in the base of Mount Eisenhower or Mount Edith Cavell, then the public is going to be barred from Jasper and Banff. But for the present we can agree with Gregory Clark: "The teeming millions of America need these sanctuaries as much as they need wealth."

After careful consideration, I believe Alberta is the most spectacular of all Canadian provinces. They say it has everything. Well, not quite. It has no salt-water fishing, and it has not a tenth enough paved roads. In an area almost as great as that of France and Germany combined (255,285 square miles) it has only 521 miles of paved roads. True, it has 2,700 miles of first-class graveled roads. And the record should show that for its population of 800,000, the province has done well in providing a total of 17,560 miles of one kind of road or another. But we are left to consider the fact that many of the finest tourist attractions either cannot be reached at all by automobile, or cannot be reached in comfort. Road building is left to the provinces, and they greatly need help from the Canadian national government.

Lacking national aid, Alberta has done what she could. The province has spent more than $20,000,000 on roads in the past two years. It continued its road-building programs in 1948, beginning work on highways between Medicine Hat and Calgary, Lloydminster and Edmonton. From the United States boundary to Edmonton, the only piece of road not paved is a short strip between Coutts and Lethbridge. New pavement has been laid from Lethbridge to Macleod and Calgary; from Calgary to Banff; from Calgary to Edmonton; and from Edmonton to Seba Beach, which is about a quarter of the distance between Edmonton and Jasper.

Even with insufficient highways and few surplus accommodations, Alberta offers unforgettable vacations: Mountain peaks which are positively magnificent, higher above the visitor's level than our own Rockies in Colorado (which are taller, but the roads are at a greater altitude), colored lakes, pastel snow, blue ice, ice-water rivers, friendly "wild" game, dude ranches, unique trailriding, miles of Alpine meadows alive with exotic flowers which cannot be matched anywhere else, luxurious hotels and remote but comfortable, interesting, and inviting lodges. All this with excellent hunting, fishing, canoeing, warm chinook winds, the largest herd of bison in the country, the Calgary Stampede, the Valley of the Dinosaurs, and the cosmic neon of the Northern Lights.

Driving across Canada you would almost certainly enter Alberta on Route 1 near Medicine Hat. But coming from the United States the best Routes are 2 and 4. First for a

tourist visit in that area is Waterton Lakes National Park,
which you reach by a short trip on Route 6. In the park,
which is 220 square miles in area and has fifty miles or so
of good roads traversing it, nature has given you mountains in technicolor. Purple, green, and gold peaks top
mountains rising right off the plain, or so it seems. To the
south is Glacier National Park, in the United States, to
the north Crows' Nest Forest Reserve, to the west the
Rockies, forming the boundary beween Alberta and British
Columbia. There are some camping sites and several excellent hotels, including the Prince of Wales, Waterton Lakes
Hotel and Chalets ($3.00 to $4.00, single, European), Bal-
linacor, and Stanley; and the Kilmorey Lodge and Crandell
Lodge.

Turn right on either Route 5 or Route 6 (you'll miss
sending a postcard from the little town of Whiskey) and
get back on Route 2, which is best for the northern trek
to Calgary and Edmonton. That Oldman River actually
exists at Macleod, which you come to next. Just a few
engine turnings away over Route 3 is Lethbridge, where
Alberta's industry began near the coal mines of Nicholas
Sheran. Sheran, an Irishman from Tenth Av-nyuh in Little
Old New York, came looking for gold but found only
the black variety: coal. There's a cairn commemorating the
first mine, but nothing to memorialize the sacrifice of the
poor suckers who must pay for coal, nowadays. (In Lethbridge: Marquis Hotel.)

Down here in the southern section of the province, the
country consists of flat plains. You'll notice as you drive to
Calgary, which is Cowtown, pahdner, that the undulating
"foothills" are almost ideal for ranching. At Nanton there's
the Trail's End Riding Camp, a dude ranch in the Porcupine Hills, as the literature says, "for those who care to
ride, hike, or loaf" ($25 a week, average, horses included;

plain and plentiful Western food). The Calgary area represents the breezy "West" to Canadians, who are just a bit shocked by the openhanded friendliness and talk of the broad-hatted, booted cowhands and ranchers. This is a favorite town for second sons of British nobility, those chaps who aren't going to be left anything but a thirst, as a patrimony. Here in the valley of the Bow you can buy drinks for a passle of 'em, if you are so minded. The Stampede, a mounted Mardi Gras with bawling cattle for mood music, is held the first part of July.

Calgary is a pretty city, and it got that way in fifty years. At the turn of the century it was pretty rough, and today they try to trade on that tradition. But, in proportion to its population, Calgary has as many pretty girls as Dallas, Texas, and that's chomping a meaningful cud, mister. (The Empire, Empress, Imperial, King Edward, Lethbridge Union, Palliser, Queen's, Royal, St. Louis, St. Regis, Victoria, Wales, York and Yale hotels.) Jack Oakie stopped in a Calgary hotel this past year while taking movie background and action scenes at the Stampede. This hotel was one of those which are nice, but too near to the railroad yards. Engines chug, chugged "through the room" all night. At an early morning hour Jack called the desk clerk and asked: "When does this room leave for Banff?"

For an interesting side trip taking you back a few million years, follow Route 1 to the right out of Calgary, then turn left on Route 9 to Drumheller, where a secondary road north takes you to the vicinity of Munson Ferry, through the Red Deer River valley to the Bad Lands Reserve and Dinosaur Park. You must walk a short distance to the fossils. I didn't, but those who have visited it tell me I missed something; that if the place looked as weird when the big beasts picked it for a burial ground, then we have an insight into the workings of the saurian mind, if that contributes anything.

Highway Number 1 continues west from Calgary to Banff. This is a good road, well paved, and a favorite with American tourists. At Cochrane, twenty-three miles west of Calgary, there is the excellent Ghost Dude Ranch. You can go there by Greyhound Bus, if you like. Ghost River Park is handy, with its beautiful lake, and there is trout fishing in the tributaries of the Bow and Ghost, not far off Route 1.

Route 2 continues north through Olds, Innisfall, and Red Deer, little places which have supplied hundreds of stories to Albertan folklore. Red Deer is the gateway to western hunting lands.

It is a short drive, now, to Edmonton, the capital. During World War II, Edmonton was a fairly large base for American forces. To them Edmonton was the Selkirk Beer Parlor, located at 101st and Jasper (right in the heart of the city), the general meeting place for all; "Mike's News Stand," operated by John "Mike" Michaels, who was a personal friend to each and every one of them; the Barn, biggest and best dance hall; the Arena, which they used to pack to the roof for sports events, particularly in the winter; and Tony's Cafe, for big, thick steaks. They will recall going "the rounds," starting at the King Edward or Royal George Hotel, where they were serving beer on the half-hour, then to the Selkirk, which would be serving on the hour, thence to the Cecil, which served almost any time, and back to the King Edward or Royal George because the minute hand had made a trip around again.

Well, Tony's Cafe has changed hands. It's now Rony's, and hasn't quite the flair that it used to have. The Barn is now a swank night club. The Arena has been refurbished and is still the home of hockey. And the jeep the United

States Military Police used to drive around, with its
wooden sides to keep out the cold—it's still there, for some
American personnel remain at the Base.

Edmonton was only observing ancient custom when she
gave a royal welcome to American soldiers. From the time
men first ventured westward and northward they enjoyed
visiting Fort Edmonton, logical transit point for the west
and north. The Hudson's Bay Company pioneers picked
the highest bank of the North Saskatchewan River for
their sprawling, stockaded fortress. Once the city spilled
out over the wood walls it just kept on, until now this
famed university and outfitters' community uses up miles
of the surrounding prairie. The first railroad came in 1891,
the Klondike gold rushers somewhat later, and, successful
or not, a high percentage of them came back only as far as
Edmonton. Casual visitors might suggest this was not because of the climate. But, if you don't like Edmonton's
climate, wait a minute. It may change as much as 40 to 50
degrees in a few hours, although this is much more likely
to happen farther south where chinook breezes blow.
Wind, rising from the Canadian Rockies, is chilled in the
upper air. Coming down the Eastern Slope it is condensed,
and in the process of compression is heated considerably,
striking the foothills as a warm, dry wind. It is because
Edmonton has medium humidity and crisp air that her
citizens say the climate is the best in the world. And perhaps that is why her doctors can almost prove (from the
death-rate figures) that the city is the most healthful in
Canada. Incidentally, the Edmonton definition of a
chinook is: "Hot air from British Columbian politicians!"

Edmonton's Chamber of Commerce claims the city is
the "Crossroads of the World." While that would seem a
trifle ebullient, it is well to note that Edmonton has come
from 7,500 population in 1914 to her present 115,000, and

that her future growth will probably be even more astounding. Right now she is the staging area for attempts to bring back the uranium at Great Bear Lake, gold at Yellowknife, furs from hundreds of thousands of square miles, oil from the MacMurray Bay area, site of the world's largest visible reserves, and oil from Leduc, half an hour's drive by automobile from Edmonton. If Americans ever can motor around the world in their own cars it is likely that they will go through Edmonton, for it was the staging area, too, for the Alaska Highway. If the time ever comes that the Russians will co-operate, a ferry over the Bering Straits, only a mile or so, will bring you to Siberia, whence you can drive to central Europe and even Africa! So that whichever way the world goes, toward peace or war, Edmonton has a mighty future. She would have one if she were nothing more than the obvious: the gateway to the Mackenzie-Athabaska country and the Peace River, distributing point for the north, air-freight depot, and northern traffic hub.

The people are vital. Though they come from a hundred different races (Edmonton has the only Moslem temple in North America, the Mosque of Al Raschid, 111th Avenue, between 101st and 102nd Streets) there is little friction and much civic pride. I liked the place very much for its spirit; I couldn't find many interesting places for ordinary tourists. There are the pleasing-looking Parliament Buildings, where they passed the "funny-money" legislation, for a new form of social credit, which hasn't done too many wonders; the George McDougall Memorial Shrine and Museum, oldest building in the city and earliest Protestant church in Alberta; and, at St. Albert, eight miles away, Father Lacombe's shrine. Father Lacombe did much to keep peace between warlike Indian tribes.

Edmonton is a great town for sports. Any winter term,

go to a high-school cloakroom and you'll find a hockey stick and skates over every hook, goalie's equipment in the corner. Sometimes one Edmonton family will turn out four or five famous hockey players. They no longer harness moose teams to sleds up there but they skate, swim, hike, and hunt.

One of the most interesting of its organizations is the unique Pioneer Gun Club. There are only ten members. An invitation to visit their hunting lodge on Big Lake, west of St. Albert, is prized by outdoorsmen like a boudoir invitation from the reigning queen in Hollywood. Just before the opening of the duck season they put on a big dinner, the preparation of which is presided over by the member who has been the leading male cook in Edmonton for a generation. There is a big, round table covered with scotch, gin, rye, bourbon, and other necessities of life, such as glasses and ice. In the center is a big, round earthenware jar. For each drink for yourself and guest, if you bring one, you toss a quarter into the bowl. For each shot at a duck you deposit a nickel for "Ducks Unlimited."

Out in the back yard there are barrels for empty bottles. One week end two members, forgetting Monday happened to be a holiday, drank rather liberally of the supplies laid in on Friday. By Monday morning they were badly in need of sustenance. It occurred to one of them that there's always a drop or two left in an "empty" bottle. So they took a tumbler and "bled" every receptacle in the throwaway heap. Gin, rye, rum, whatever. It filled the tumbler. Then they rationed drinks until sundown, and with great ceremony tossed off the final jiggers. At that second another member drove up with fresh, potable rations. Later this pair went to St. Cloud for a shave. The barber wasn't in, so one shaved the other. In the meantime a Russian farmer with a beard about a month old came in. So they shaved him, one keeping apprehensive eyes on the door in the fear that any moment the barber might return.

While the tourist probably will never be able to wangle an invitation from the Pioneer Gun Club, he can sign on with the Trailer Riders, an organization we will describe when we get to Banff, or with the Canadian Alpine Club, for those who like to climb. Both of these organizations are well equipped and provide excellent food and sleeping accommodations. The tenderfeet among you can enjoy their activities, too.

Though the road is more for jeep travel than for regular automobiles, you may drive north to Athabasca, around the southern fringe of Lesser Slave Lake and up to Peace River Crossing. At the confluence of the Smoky and the Peace, high on a hill with a remarkable view, there's a cairn which commemorates a man and a legend. "Twelve-foot" Davis is the man. He had gone to the Yukon and taken the last twelve feet available along a producing strip —and struck it rich. Coming back up the Peace River by canoe he had found his idyllic spot, built a cabin, and spent the remainder of his life working for, and giving to, others.

The Peace River valley is incredibly fertile. The river winds through green garden plots half-crescented by hills. This is the Ohio valley of the north, only much bigger. Here, as in the Ohio valley, there is much coal and gas underneath the soil. Winters are long, but the summers are rewarding. However, unless you are hunting or fishing or on your way to the Alaska Highway (which we'll discuss later) I don't know why you would be up there. (Mc-Namara and Victory Hotels.) The road dips south to Grande Prairie, then north and west again to cross into British Columbia and link up with the beginning of the Alaska Highway, at Dawson Creek.

Route 16 from Edmonton east takes you to Elk Island Park, just thirty miles from the capital. They have more than one thousand bison fenced in there, with only fifty-one square miles in which to roam. You may camp or swim or hike but there are no hotels or tourist courts. Route 16 west takes you to what many persons, myself included, believe to be the finest tourist attraction on this continent: Jasper National Park. After paying a modest car fee of $2.00, you enter the park and the scenery starts right away. Let's hope the driver of your car isn't too emotional about lovely and soul-shattering views, or he may drive off the road, ohing, ahing, and gesticulating. It has been done before. A friend of mine even did it at night for the same reason—in Bing Crosby's car. You come in along the route of the Athabasca River, the way the first explorers did. The ice-capped mountains seem terrifyingly high, frighteningly close, chillingly cold, and seemingly possessed of radiating strength. It is as though you were to be allowed a cosmic revelation never before made; that you were close to Nature, which has just done something big. Coming from the eastern provinces, you have left the oldest rocks in the world for some of the newest great rock masses. You wouldn't think such a few million years would make any difference; but to me it was the awareness of this difference, coupled with the spectacular colorings, which sent thrilling chills coursing spinewards.

When you arrive in Jasper you notice that it is a small town, carefully laid out, with a neat stone Park Headquarters and post office, and that the mountains seem to encircle the town. You wonder what the view will be like from your hotel room. And the next thing you invariably do is go over and look at the totem poles. They're down next to the railroad station, and they're spectacular, as befits a spectacular place.

I stayed at the Athabasca Hotel because the Jasper Lodge was officially closed, although a few of the staff were around waiting for Bing Crosby to return from a hunting trip. Mr. Crosby had just won the Totem Pole Golf Tournament with a finish so thrilling I accused him of having a special script written for it. Anyway, he brought with him one of the best script writers in the business, the producer of his radio show, Bill Morrow. Morrow, moonfaced and full of fun, unassuming and easy to know, seemed the perfect companion for the guy who wears so well on the screen. Jasper was ideal for Mr. Crosby because the people didn't act like maniacs simply because they recognized him. They spoke and went on about their business. Yet I noted when I rode with Bill in Mr. Crosby's car that the girls had it spotted, even the Indian girls. You saw many Indian girls, but never an Indian boy, on the streets of Jasper.

Mr. Crosby's fans might feel slighted if I failed to tell a little story or two about him. One day the waitress brought him loose tea leaves in the cup and then poured hot water on them. "Take these back," said Mr. Crosby with mock severity. "These leaves are for readin', not drinkin'." And when they asked for a speech after presenting the golf cup, Mr. Crosby related how a certain Mr. Hope also played golf; how in Scotland he carefully selected a caddy who wouldn't lose golf balls.

"You sure you always find the balls?" asked Mr. Hope.

"Aye," replied the ancient mariner of the fairways.

"Well, find one and let's get going," said Mr. Hope, as reported by Mr. Crosby.

When "Der Bingle" hit the trail it may have been to try to shoot big game, or it may have been to get away from the bears around Jasper. They are everywhere. We drove out to the city dump and counted fourteen in view at once. Bill Ruddy, of the Park Department, who was nice enough to drive me around during my stay, once took a snapshot with twenty-two of them in focus. "Twenty-two bears and my mother-in-law," said Bill.

I was at the telegraph office one night when the track-man came up to the station pell-mell. Three bears had disputed the Canadian National right of way with him. Over at Jasper Lodge, Jack Stark, the manager who worked his way up from bellhop in that same hotel, showed me around and told me bears break into the $20-a-day cabins, being smart enough not to bother with the cheaper ones, and get into the space between the foundation and the water pipes, which are kept warm so they won't freeze and burst. There the bears hibernate. One winter the management turned on heat for some visiting Boy Scouts from England and the bears, thinking it was spring, came out, rubbing their eyes. There was no peace with those bears that year because for three months they acted like a man waked up in the middle of the night. Mr. Stark told me the lodge used to have imitation acorns on its blind strings, but upon opening each summer they'd find the squirrels had clipped them and stacked them in sugar bowls in the basement.

I saw the beautiful, rustic design of the lodge, marveled at the hat check room made of diseased tree branches twisted by their malady into interesting shapes (I later saw the valley where all the trees grow like this), and the lodge used by the present King and Queen of England on their trip to Canada just before the war. It was very comfortable but there was nothing unique about it.

Bill Ruddy took me on many trips about the park, and I hope you will let nothing dissuade you from the same, especially the jaunt into Maligne Lake, perhaps the most enticing spot on earth. Bill showed me Dead Man's Hole, which seems to have no bottom. We went to the Lookout,

on the way to visit the Angel glacier at Mount Edith
Cavell. Here is a view in many ways more impressive than
the Grand Canyon. Not so immense. Not to be compared
in size. But with the ice-water river in it and cool caps
around it, huge, colorful, and alive. Just the day before,
Bill had seen a grizzly crossing the stream in front of him,
a fellow about ten feet tall and with a head a foot and
a half wide. We didn't have any luck with grizzlies, but we
saw herds of deer and elk and quite a few moose. Bill had
given me a copy of the ancient papers of the first explorers
to these parts, and it pleased me to find a moose (with hundreds more around) on approximately the same spot where
Captain John Palliser had noted the last tired moose remaining in the entire area, in 1859. Things were so bad
then that when an Indian named Tekarra shot badly
needed meat they named a mountain after him.

I suppose now that Bing won the golf tournament and
made a picture at Jasper, they'll change the spelling of
"Byng Pass."

As we rode toward Mount Edith Cavell, Bill told me
the story of Mrs. Slark, who came up there years ago with
her husband. He left her at a spot near the foot of the
Angel glacier, went exploring over the ice, and never
came back. Knowing that he had fallen into a crevasse, she
waited over the months and years for his body to be washed
down, so she could bury him. At the spot where she waited
she built a tea room, which is there yet. Mrs. Slark only
gave up a year or so ago. The story of her devotion should
be brought home to our trial brides of these I'm-Wed-
While-It's-Convenient days.

A patch of an acre or so of ice seemed to be on the verge
of falling off the cap. I said so and Bill replied: "People
have been waiting for that piece to fall for forty years."
This blue ice some millions of years old was subject to

melting and change but it hadn't changed much, probably, from the night it reflected the same starlight under which Christ was born.

There's much to see and do in Jasper, summer and winter. You could spend months exploring in the summer, or skiing in winter. The absolute best in Canadian skiing is found in the Canadian Rockies. Powder snow lies a foot deep. Mile-wide downhill slopes dip beautifully as much as three miles. Some stretches are as steep as 40 degrees. I read a pamphlet once which said: "You can start pointing your skis downhill near the 8,500-foot level and wind up alongside a chalet at timber line." The Whistlers, near the city, is a favorite course; sort of rough for novices, though.

I could easily write this entire book about the alpine plateaus full of flowers; the mountain goats and the sand they like to lick, although it's not salt (something different in it; probably should be analyzed to pep up your breakfast food); the various peaks and lakes; and the upper reaches of Blue Creek Valley, with its natural arch, blood-red peaks, and pink shale slopes. But we must get on, and you must actually see Jasper; you'll not be complete as a person until you've seen, and felt, and adopted your own nook of this 4,200-square-mile area, literally the scenic tops.

To get about it would be better if you had your own car or could persuade a native to drive you in his. Otherwise, there are two good guided-tour services, one from the Lodge and the other from the Athabasca. This latter hotel, by the way, is moderate in rates, managed by very reasonable folks, serves good food, but has paper-thin walls. The Lodge is on the American plan, so the difference in price is not so great as you might think. Nothing can quite compare with its beautiful situation on Lac Beauvert, unless it would be the view from Rocke Bonhomme Bungalows, set in the woods and with million-year-old ice water flowing right in front of it, just beyond the road. The Athabasca is so dependent upon glacier meltings that the river will be several inches higher in the afternoon following a hot morning. Except for the horrible name, Kiefer's Kozy Kabins are very nice. I also recommend Tekarra Lodge and Pine Bungalow Cabins, outside of Jasper, for those with their own cars. In town, besides the Athabasca, the Astoria and Pyramid hotels are fair.

After you have visited Jasper you will agree with Captain Palliser that: "Here is an impressible, ethereal, and esthetic influence of a vast panorama of solitudes, beautiful lakes, deep canyons, dense forests, and magnificent valleys with pure air, a whole which inspires, elevates, and dignifies all who come under the spell of nature."

And with Sir Arthur Conan Doyle, who in his "The Athabasca Trail" wrote:

I shall hear the roar of rivers where the rapids foam and tear,
I shall smell the virgin upland with its balsam-laden air,
And shall dream that I am riding down the winding woody vale,
With the packer and the packhorse on the Athabasca Trail.

The ride from Jasper to Banff is above par and sometimes above the clouds. Truly a "high" way, its 189 miles include a couple of the scenic wonders of the world. You can drive it in eight hours, gawking time, or go by guided tour. This drive follows wide-sweeping switchbacks to 2,000 feet or so above the valley floor, with Nature doing her best in changing the picture, and affording views of the mountains: Signal, Tekarra, Kerkeslin, Hardisty, Franchere, the Throne, and Edith Cavell, nee Giekie. You go on up the Athabasca to Athabasca, Sunwapta, and Tanglewood Falls—and this is the core of the Canadian Rockies—to the most impressive ice field outside the Arctic Circle. The majestic grandeur of this massive icecap at the Roof of the World puts a frost on almost any other spot you'll visit. There are 110 square miles of blue-white ice, and from here, rivers start on their way to three oceans —the Atlantic, Pacific, and Arctic. Lunch at the Columbia Icefield Chalet. If proper facilities were provided could you not ski here in summer, even mid-summer? But we haven't time to ponder. We're off, now, for the most famous single pool in the Rockies, Lake Louise, but perhaps stopping for views of numerous lakes along the way, and at the Mistaya River Valley; right from the road you will have been able to see the mighty Athabasca glacier— with some member of your party quipping: "The Ice Man Cometh." Now Mount Eisenhower (and if the tourists don't stop taking souvenir hunks of it there'll be only a minor rock pile left), Johnston Canyon, and down the Bow Valley to Banff.

Lake Louise is a perfect little mirror lake, surrounded by great mountain peaks, and other lakes compare to it the way black-and-white movies of the Fatty Arbuckle days compare to modern technicolor films. That's Mount Victoria sitting massively back there with the heavy white shawl. Facing the lake is Chateau Lake Louise ($8.00 up, single, European), Mt. Temple View Bungalow Camp ($3.00 to $4.00, double, European), Mountain Inn, Deer Lodge, Triangle Inn, Inglenook Lodge and Cabins, and Paradise Bungalow Camp. Mountain Inn and Lake Louise Ski Lodge are open during the winter, ordinarily. The Ptarmigan-Skoki region, north of Lake Louise, is good for alpine skiing, with accommodations at Temple Chalet, five miles from the lake, and Skoki Lodge, six miles north.

It is almost unnecessary to remind you that from Lake Louise you can hike and ride and swim and fish. Favorite trips from here are to the Plain of Six Glaciers, near by; to the Lake in the Clouds and Lakes Mirror and Agnes, which lie in cirques 6,800 feet above sea level; and to Moraine Lake, in the Valley of Ten Peaks. Moraine Lake's hues are of sapphire and emerald. The peaks originally bore the names of the ten numerals of the Stony Indian language.

At Banff, it naturally depends upon the attraction the place has for you as to where you'll stay. If you just want to be in the swim and can afford it, the impressive Banff Springs Hotel is the place to go. From its terrace you may see those smart people you saw a month or so before at the Gran Hotel Reforma in Mexico City, or the Chateau Frontenac, or the Waldorf-Astoria. It has a hot-water swimming pool and a golf course complete with undulating terrain, well-placed hazards, tricky crosswinds and its own fans— from all over the world. The course is at 4,500 feet above sea level. Here the Trail Riders of the Canadian Rockies make up their tenderfoot posses to ride out and capture adventure. (Five days cost $55.) When they come back they put on the acts with which they wowed each other around the campfires, and townspeople and other tourists "catch" the show at the sports grounds of the Banff Springs. At least they did last year. There are over a thousand miles of trail leading to such places as Mount Assiniboine, Spray Lakes, Simpson Pass, Skoki Valley, Lake O'Hara, Snow Creek, Panther Lake, and Harrison Lake. The Sky Line Trail Hikers and the Canadian Youth Hostelers, both international go-and-see-it organizations, conduct annual excursions, always worth while and almost professionally thorough. The Alpine Club, previously noted, has a building here, and now and again you might see a renowned mountain buster walking the streets of Banff. Looking down on Banff is Mount Norquay, described as "the answer to a skiing tournament official's prayers." There is a downhill course two miles long, sporting a vertical drop of 2,800

Typical of the prairie country, this spot is near Edmonton, Alberta.

The Davis Grave is an historic landmark at Peace River, Alberta.

Riding enthusiasts in Canadian Rockies camp in tepees, ride trail over rugged terrain.

Majestic Mount Kerkeslin
in Jasper National Park.

Stern east face of Mount
Charlton, towering above
Maligne Lake in Alberta.

A tourist's-eye view of Mount Edith Cavell in Jasper National Park.

Glacier of the Angel, Mount Edith Cavell.

The Bastion is a familiar sight to Jasper National Park trail hikers.

Trail hikers of the Canadian Rockies hold annual camp in Banff.

Tall tales are told around the campfire at night.

Snow-capped Cascade Mountain as it looks from the entrance to
Banff National Park's Administration Building, Banff, Alberta.

British Columbia's turbulent Bulkley River rushes through Bulkley Gate.

Highest peak in the Canadian Rockies is Mount Robson, British Columbia.

feet. The maximum gradient is 45 degrees. Also, they have a ski tow and near-by practice slopes for beginners. And, on the other end of the thermostat, the hot mineral baths, discovery of which first attracted attention to this area and together with its magnificent scenery caused it to be set aside as Canada's first national park, are still there and much in use.

Gone now is Jim Brewster, the Canadian tour tycoon who was sort of a cross between Tom Mix and Will Rogers, and canny enough to develop things like Trail Riders, and Indian Days. He played host to kings, chorus girls, and the new royalty, atomic bomb scientists and Broadway touts alike. And everyone liked him. The film *So This Is London*, which starred Will Rogers, was made from a script which followed Brewster's adventures when he was a guest of the Earl of Suffolk, in England. He was a real businessman, and every time he wore chaps the tourist rate went up fifty cents a day, but he gave them all their money's worth in atmosphere.

In the old days in Banff, another popular personality was Louie Wong, who established a plain but clean restaurant and religiously sent twenty-dollar gold pieces back to Canton, China. In his front windows, after the custom of the times, he heaped mounds of fruit. One day the Great Bolderedo, a traveling prestidigitator, came to town and amazed a large audience with feats of legerdemain. After the show, but minus his beard, he went with friends to Wong's for steak. On the way out his glance fell upon the neatly piled oranges. He bought six.

"Think I'll eat one now," he said, and taking a pocket knife, split the fruit. Out rolled a twenty-dollar gold piece. In apparent amazement he opened the other five, to discover a gold piece in the center of each. "Strangest oranges I've ever seen," said Bolderedo as he pocketed the knife and walked out of the restaurant. Then he and his friends strolled across the street and stood for twenty minutes watching Louie Wong get a sharp carving knife and open every orange left in that huge California shipment.

You won't find many Banff businessmen as gullible as Louie Wong, these days. The town is well developed along business lines. Almost any class of accommodation is available, too. Hotels include the Cascade, Homestead, Hot Springs, King Edward, and the excellent Mount Royal. Then there are Becker's Bungalows (two of these), Scratch's, Mountview, Pinewood and Fairholme bungalows, and Sunshine Lodge. There are Mount Eisenhower Lodge and Mount Eisenhower Bungalow Camp near the forks and the eminence named after the president of Columbia University.

Route 1, the Trans-Canada Highway, which we mentioned as the best way of crossing the province, comes in at Medicine Hat, the center of ranching and flour milling down in the southeastern section of the province (Cecil and Cosmopolitan Hotels), goes on through Calgary, and then enters the Banff Park and turns west at Lake Louise to go over the Great Divide into Yoho (which means "wonderful" in Indian talk) National Park. Since white men have visited these regions they have made the Great Divide a meeting place. In the Jasper-Banff parks there is a pool called the Punch Bowl, where the pack trains would meet, exchange news, freight, and gossip, and have a drink as a regular ceremony. So that instead of meaning a place of sad and final parting, as it does all over the world, in Alberta the term "Great Divide" takes on a cheerful connotation. And that is fitting because Alberta, already intriguing, compelling and winning, is destined to become host to the traveling masses instead of the well-heeled classes as roads and landing fields improve so that distance becomes even less important than it is today.

· 14 ·

England, California,
and Switzerland, Combined

Were I an intending immigrant, I would risk a good deal
of discomfort to get on the land in British Columbia; and
were I rich, with no attachments outside England, I would
swiftly buy me a farm or a house in that country for the
mere joy in it.—RUDYARD KIPLING.

Take the best parts of California: the giant trees, the
winter climate, and the eternal fountain of optimism, and
eschew cults, exhibitionists, and the lunatic fringe; add
Switzerland's mountains, meadows, and general aura of
freshness; and people this charming land with the best of
England, leavened with a sprinkling of the interesting and
energetic from the remainder of the world, and you will
have British Columbia.

It is Canada's third largest province, 50,000 square miles
greater in area than the combined states of California,
Oregon, and Washington. It counts only two persons to the
square mile, but that fact is misleading, for Vancouver, the
Dominion's third city, accounts for approximately half
the provincial population; and fully 75 per cent of all
British Columbians live in cities and towns.

The province leads the entire Dominion in per-capita
wealth, per-capita purchasing power and per-capita production. Americans visiting it will find verdant meadow-
lands and valleys giving way to snow-capped peaks of
stunning stateliness, lambent lakes, frowning canyons,
plunging rivers, and scores of miles of fragrant trees. They
will find, too, the climate they are seeking when they mis-
takenly head their cars toward California in the summer-

time. Great areas of the province cannot be reached by automobile, but the two great railway systems provide the best in service, both by Pullman and by boat.

Accommodations range from one of the most interesting of hotels on earth to a crofter's lean-to in the mountains, but the hostelries are neither the best nor the worst in Canada. Not even the gushiest female guidebook author could call British Columbia "quaint," a fact which rather leaves them faint. But you may drive in the space of a few hours from a very modern city to a hick town decked out with totem poles. It is unfortunate that the loveliest, most exciting area, that of the middle and north ocean coasts, with its submerged mountains forming heavily wooded bastions in a great protective chain, cannot be visited except by boat or plane. For here the dense forest is magnificent, the finest softwood stand in the British Empire. Here the humid atmosphere is pleasing, fish and game are prodigious.

British Columbia's climate is varied, yet the mildest Canada affords. In the inland central section the air is much drier than on the coast, rainfall is slight, and irrigation necessary. Summer is a great deal warmer than on the coast, where there is much rainfall, but winters are considerably colder, and where there is snow in inches in Vancouver, this inland section has it in feet—sometimes even a hundred feet in a year.

Topographically, the country is rugged. Back in those millions of years ago that geologists bandy about so freely, the great icecap gouged out wide trenches, today's well-watered valleys, and carved out stubborn ridges, today's peaks. The Rocky Mountains, the chain farthest east, the one which, at the Great Divide, forms the boundary between Alberta and British Columbia, sets the pattern. It runs roughly parallel to the coast, and three other chains

line up, until the fourth, the Coast Range, winds up partially in the Pacific Ocean.

One of the factors likely to detract from British Columbia as a restful vacation site is the fact that so many Americans will be discovering and investigating business oppor-
tunities there. The province is comparatively new, when
extensive settlement is considered. Its discovery goes back
at least as far as Sir Francis Drake, but it wasn't until the
Spanish got interested that England asserted her claim.
Then after she got it, she wasn't interested, until Americans came over the line, first for furs and later for gold.

Meanwhile, British Columbians, who had dealt mostly
with the Orient and California, very nearly voted to join
the United States. Prince Edward Island, where confederation of the Canadian provinces was first outlined, was very
far away, indeed—over the Rockies and thousands of miles
away. It was the promise of the railroad, a link with the
remainder of Canada, which took the trick. When the
railroad got out there, in 1885, Vancouver looked something like our depression "Hoover" cities, with a population around 2,000. In sixty-three years it has developed
from an isolated outpost to the position of the world's
chief grain port, and is straining toward becoming Canada's greatest port. Opening of the Panama Canal made
the shipping of lumber practical for British Columbia.
Now Vancouver is on the march, and seems destined to
become one of the world's truly great cities; some who
toboggan on economic indices say world trade is shifting
from the Atlantic to the Pacific, that the largest city on
the North American continent will be there; that, further-
more, it may be Vancouver.

Entrance to British Columbia is easy. Besides Route 2,
previously mentioned as entering the province and linking
with the beginning of the Alaska Highway at Dawson

Creek, the Trans-Canada Highway, Route 1, goes over the Great Divide, connecting up at Golden with Route 4, which drives straight south to the American border. One continues around the Big Bend and through some of the most colorful country in the province, down to Vancouver —even across to Vancouver Island and up north, where it flaps to a finish on Salmon River. A number of good roads enter British Columbia from the United States. First among them is Route 99 from Seattle, which runs into the Trans-Canada Highway near Vancouver. Good, also, are Routes 97 and 4, and from Spokane, 395 (linking up with Route 22) and 195 (linking up with Route 6); from Montana, Routes 95 and 93.

There are excellent boat, bus, and plane connections from Seattle to Vancouver, and the Northern Pacific Railroad provides up-to-date service by rail. Some boat connections between the two cities also include Victoria.

I made my entrance, on this latest trip to the province, on the Canadian National Railway from Jasper. Bill Morrow, Mr. Crosby's radio producer, was with me, and we discovered on the train the Sutherlands, Elliot and his wife, whom I hadn't seen since they entertained me so handsomely back in New Glasgow, Nova Scotia. The view from the observation windows kept us busy. You cross into British Columbia at Yellowhead Pass, which gets its name from François Decoigne, a French-Canadian everyone could have forgotten—except that he had noisy, corn-colored hair. Because of that a pass, a lake, a mountain and *Tête Jaune Cache* got their names. François, a fur trapper, worked these parts, and it seems everyone who passed this way made a note of that blazing thatch. Yellowhead Pass is one of the most famous on the continent. It crosses the Rockies at 3,713 feet, which is lower than any other, and for this reason it has been in use for more than a century.

At its crest only a few feet separate the headwaters of the Fraser River, flowing to the Pacific, from those of the Miette, which eventually reach the Arctic. On the right-hand side of the track rises Yellowhead Mountain. Its serrated crest is known as the Seven Sisters.

Now we followed the Fraser River, named after Simon Fraser, who in 1808 explored it to its source, high in the Rockies. For most of its 695 miles its mad passage through rocky gorges seems to have concentrated all the wild emotion of the peaks, glaciers, and trackless forests in which it found life. At Rainbow we saw several streams pouring down from the hillsides into Moose Lake, a widening of the Fraser, eight miles long, deep sapphire to light emerald, etching many a peak in reverse in its still depths. At Red Pass, just beyond the lake, the Canadian National Railways splits, one line going to Prince Rupert and the other south to Vancouver. And soon we were treated to the rarest view in the Rockies—that of Mount Robson. The train came to a stop and at once a hundred amateur photographers got out and shot pictures. I couldn't guess how many feet Bill Morrow shot, but the Eastman people must have had to put on another shift.

It seems singular that now nobody can remember who Robson was, this chap for whom the greatest bump of them all, 12,972 feet, is named. On its well-shaped head there is a silver helmet of ice. You see the south side of the mountain from the railway line. Getting to the opposite and more beautiful side calls for a horseback ride of sixteen miles. But three glaciers drape themselves down that side, and one, Tumbling Glacier, ends in a precipice from which huge chunks thunder into the emerald lake below. Along the west side of the mountain runs a deep, lush valley into which waterfalls cascade on every hand, the Valley of a Thousand Falls.

Near Jackman, the Fraser River again, turquoise and impatient for its rendezvous with salt water, and then to the right the Cariboo Mountains, most of them named after Prime Ministers, and cold and wet in the upper story. Now the line runs through the Canoe River Valley, climbing to the summit of Albreda Pass. Off to the left you look down this valley's length, and across a vast green carpet there is the river's silvery thread dropped by a careless hand.

At Pyramid the train went so close to the falls that the cars were wet by the spray. The water comes down the mountainside in three splashes, which Morrow and I called "Tinker to Evers to Chance."

There was a touch of human interest at Blue River. The flower garden at the station has been built by the travelers of the world for the stationmaster's wife. She laid it out, planted it, and produced a touch of beauty so different from the customary cinder-and-standpipe view that travelers who know about it, particularly those making a round trip, hustle off and do some planting in the garden. You can do it too, and if you tell the conductor what you're up to, you needn't be in a hurry. Mountains around the village are snow-capped and striking in appearance. This little spot is a favorite stepping-down place for those who would visit Wells Gray Park, 1,800 square miles in area.

Kamloops, gateway to the Okanagan Valley, justly renowned for fruit growing, and center of dozens of fine lakes more or less full of Kamloops trout, is next. Sometimes during the summer other lakes become fished out, but not here. (In the Kamloops area: Cornwall Lodge, Bar C Guest Ranch, Echo Lodge, Hyas Lake, Kamloops Tourist Camp, Le Jeune Lodge, Mile High Fishing and Hunting Camp, Ltd.—we hope it's not the hunting that is limited—Peterhope Fishing Camp, which advertises itself as the place "where the fish are mad," Scott's Motel, Surrey and Sussex Lakes, West End Auto Camp.)

When we discuss a trip over the famous Cariboo Trail, we'll be back and take up these towns. But on the train trip the next thing to look for is Hell's Gate on the Fraser, south of Boston Bar. Here the waters of the mighty Fraser are jammed into a canyon a hundred feet wide. The result is more noise and froth and a much prettier sight than a convention of Southern senators. Now in a few hours you are in Vancouver, only fifteen miles due north of the United States boundary.

Vancouver is essentially "all business," yet you may enjoy a delightful vacation there. The city's life centers about the harbor because it is a very important port, and ships from fifty different lines arrive, unload, load, and sail daily. Nearly everyone you meet is making "just a quick business trip," and the hotels seem to be pretty full almost all the time. Bill Morrow and I stayed in a tiny section of the Hotel Vancouver's royal suite, there being no royalty around at the moment. (Other hotels: Georgia, Grosvenor, Devonshire, York, Castle, Belmont, Angelus, and Alcazar.)

Vancouver is a first-class city. Yet it points up, as few cities do, the fact that nature has done so much for Canada and man has done, comparatively, so little. No city could live up to nature's backdrop for Vancouver. New York's skyscrapers would be breathtaking there, though, against the flowing greenery, the great sweep of the sea and the spectacular blue-green mountains, white on top. Vancouver is a northern Rio, more spectacular even than Rio, in its northern way.

There are miles and miles of beaches, scores of interesting boat trips on fiord-like inland waters, excursions up Howe Sound, to Bowen Island (Bowen Inn) and Gambier

Island (Glen Olbee Resort). And actually a part of the city is Stanley Park, the entire western peninsula set aside for public pleasure. It's nine miles around the park; you should walk about Lost Lagoon, then drive to Lumberman's Arch, complete with totem poles, and to Prospect Point, which is high above the entrance to Burrard's Inlet. You can see liners, freighters, and tugs passing under the largest suspension bridge in the British Empire. Or take a walk down the cool nave of very tall trees to Beaver Lake.

The city has plenty of movies and smart shops (I went with Mr. Morrow while he bought some loud plaid shirts for Mr. Crosby), a Chinatown with some good restaurants, the Vancouver Club, and even a colony of turbaned, black-bearded Hindus.

The second leg of the triangle trip suggested is by sea, Vancouver to Prince Rupert. Both railway systems were having new boats built (although the Canadian Pacific seemed better off on this service than the Canadian National, at war's end) and they will have new schedules, new informative literature, by the time you read this. At any rate, the trip is almost always a smooth sea voyage, because the route is protected by a long chain of islands—except for the Queen Charlotte Sound strip, which takes only about two hours. On that part of the voyage, you'll see the entrance way to Bella Coola, which, my spies report, our High Command believed had been selected by the Japs for their first invasion point on the North American mainland. A bit farther on is Laredo Sound, which like my home town in Texas, was named after Laredo, Spain.

Prince Rupert is refreshing and different. An exceedingly well laid-out town, a day or so may happily be spent seeing its parks, with their excellent collection of totems (there are enough of them so that you can be certain to find one whose "low man" looks like Uncle Elmer), and its museum and musty old Indian handicraft and curio shops. (Prince Rupert, Central, Commercial, New Royal, Knox and Old Empress Hotels.)

Only the boats, airplanes, and trains serve Prince Rupert. Leaving there on the third side of the triangle which takes us back to Jasper, we begin the crossing of five successive valleys, the Skeena, the Bulkley, the Endako, the Nechako, and the Fraser. If by now all this is somewhat familiar to you, it will be none the less interesting and memorable. Leaving the Skeena, guarded by eternal hills, you pass through fishing villages and cannery whistle stops. At Kitwanga, the Indians are saying it with totems, spelling out family histories, using termites as erasers, I suppose.

After Hazelton, which is an authentic Indian trading post, come the valley of the Bulkley, and its formidable Gate, where the waters have carved patterns in solid rock. Spawning fish are to get an assist up this section of the river through a unique engineering feat—not escalators but something approaching them in liquid form. After you leave McBride the great mountains will keep you craning your necks, coming into view one by one, until here is Mount Robson again, and soon you are going down into Jasper.

Now for a quick trip around the province on Route 1, the Trans-Canada Highway, then on to Victoria Island, after which we'll "do" the Cariboo before considering the possibilities inherent in the Alaska Highway.

· 15 ·

Big Bend, Cariboo, and Points North

NO MATTER what may have been said about the condition of the Trans-Canada Highway, from time to time, there isn't anyone in his right mind who can deny it has plenty of scenery to offer. The section of it which begins as you enter British Columbia by crossing the Great Divide from Banff Park is an underlined case in point. For you begin with Yoho Park, and continue around the Big Bend, dip into the pretty Okanagan Valley and go to the base of the storied Cariboo Trail, on your way to Vancouver.

Yoho National Park, like that of Banff, owes its existence to the construction of the Canadian Pacific Railway, which operates a scenic line through all this striking country, down to Vancouver. If you are driving you will want to stay at the railroad's chalets or bungalow lodges at Emerald Lake, Lake O'Hara, Wapta Lake, or Yoho Valley.

The Kicking Horse Trail, as the main road is called, provides a scenic drive of thirty-five miles or so through the mountains and valleys, many of them set with lakes which rival Louise. From this road other routes branch off to special lakes, such as Emerald. After leaving Kicking Horse Pass, which got its name from what a horse did to the discoverer, Sir James Hector, when he was discovery bent (over), the road skirts Wapta Lake. This pool is the headwater of the Kicking Horse River, a fine fishing stream.

The road clings to Mount Cathedral's lower slopes, providing excellent views of the Yoho and Kicking Horse valleys,

178

then crosses the river and follows along its course to Field. This town, at the foot of Mount Stephen, is a base for the roads and trails to Yoho Valley (Yoho Valley Lodge) and various other attractions. It has churches, stores, filling stations, a Y.M.C.A., and tourist courts, as well as a public campgrounds. Lake O'Hara and Lake Emerald can be reached from Field, the latter pretty enough for anybody's calendar, any time. (Emerald Lake Chalet.)

Following the lower canyon of the Kicking Horse to where it runs into the Columbia River brings you to Golden, the town with an untarnished view. It is the center of large lumbering and mining interests and the grocery store for the Windermere Valley to the south. (Golden Lodge, Riverside and Rolston's Auto Camps and Swiss Village Camp.)

If you'll look at the map at Golden you'll see where the Big Bend got its name. The Columbia River flows north for 190 miles and then swings around and heads south for 270 miles before it shifts its allegiance to the United States flag. In that great arrowhead lie the Selkirk Mountains, Glacier National Park, and a mountain and a creek bearing my family name but, unfortunately, named for another Carnes.

This whole area is magnificent—one great scenic park. It is fairly new to tourists, having been opened to them only with this section of the Trans-Canada Highway. Row on row of peaks pop into view from the never-never land beyond the horizon. The river sheds a diaphanous veil, like an impatient virgin, in Surprise Rapids, then drops quietly into Kinbasket Lake, to make a hurried exit for the chutes of "Twenty-One Mile" where cliff faces cliff across the hurtling current. Thus to the bend, where first intrepid fur traders and explorers met by appointment like this: "I'll see you at the Boat Encampment in the summer of 1830." A fellow had to be fairly intrepid even to visit this Forest of the Gods back in those days, but year after year visiting numbers swelled and then in 1865, with thousands of Civil War ex-GI's hanging around street corners in the United States, someone discovered gold lying right out in the river here, and in one or two near-by creeks, and the human dam burst. There is a long-abandoned trail from the head of Shuswap Lake where, even today, you can see debris left in the wake of that gold-hungry mob. At any rate the excitement didn't last long; the surface gold and the hysteria vanished the following year. At Boat Encampment there's a gasoline station, a restaurant, and rooms, all simply known as "The Boat Encampment."

It is a hundred miles to the next town, Revelstoke, so you had better be sure you have the fuels and the lubricants necessary. You cross Goldstream, and the name tells you its story, then Carnes Creek, named for D. D. Carnes, Canadian geologist who discovered it; then you follow the alternate rapids and still running waters of the river to Revelstoke, a railroad town, not very large, but ringed by photogenic mountains. The largest of these bears the name of the town, and, time permitting, a drive up its side is very much worth while. Its slopes are excellent for skiing, too. (In Revelstoke: Big Auto Camp, Downie Creek Auto Courts, Duncan's Revelstoke Cabin Camp, Elliott Tourist Camp, Log Cabin Camp, and, eighteen miles away in Mount Revelstoke National Park, Heather Lodge.) This drive over Route 1 will indicate to the discerning tourist what is meant by the phrase "British Columbia has a great future in the extractive industries." This doesn't refer to extracting money from tourists but to taking raw materials from the soil and sea. Anyway, here is scenery as good as it was a hundred years ago and better than it was eighty-two years ago, when things were cluttered up by "the men who moil for gold."

You may turn directly south for Arrow Lakes, starting point of several interesting boat trips, or continue through

Eagle Pass for the Okanagan Valley, the Cariboo, and the coast. Between Revelstoke and Sicamous is the Monashee mountain system, with Mount Begbie a standout. At Sicamous, on the shore of the Shuswap, travelers by both automobile and the Canadian Pacific Railway frequently stop over, so as to save the canyon scenery ahead for daylight travel (Sicamous Hotel, Fort Gillis Auto Court, U.I. Cabins).

Salmon Arm, situated on a long arm of Shuswap Lake, reminds you of Scotland, and it is as important as New York City if you happen to be a fisherman; because at this point the lake is popularly supposed to have more fish—trout, steelhead, and landlocked salmon—than any other waters in British Columbia. Much has been written of the "sage" through here, and of the dryland belt. But having come from a land of sere grass and prickly pear, the real *brasada* country, this looked ten times more lush, more like heather, to me. (At Salmon Arm: Glen Echo Beach and Auto Park, Lakeview Cabins.) At Notch Hill the Shuswap Narrows Fishing Lodge sends a car to meet the Canadian Pacific Railway and take guests to their fishing paradise on Eagle Bay (American plan, $5 daily). Chase, which has only six hundred permanent population, sees twice that number of hunters in a few days of the season each year.

Now Kamloops, which we have discussed, and the Thompson River widens into Kamloops Lake, placid, colorful, splendid. Ashcroft, which used to be the little roaring hell of a town when the gold rush was on, has settled down to producing potatoes, and is making more money at it. The Ashcroft Manor here is the oldest "stopping house" on the Cariboo Trail from Vancouver to Kamloops. (Other places to stay: Highland Valley Lodge, J. T. Guest Ranch.)

The course turns due south along the Thompson, through Spence's Bridge, a Saturday-night town, and there's a thrill in the Thompson Canyon as you wonder whether you—that is the highway, the railroad tracks, and the river—can all get in that narrow space choked by the mountains. Botanie Crag, its green granite crest hanging over many-colored rocks, is a sight worth going out of your way to see, and then you are in the flower-bedecked plateau which gives you Lytton (Brophy, Gladwin, and Lytton auto courts). This once was favorite upping-stone to the Cariboo Road. Below here the Thompson joins the Fraser, British Columbia's mightiest stream, which, like the Thompson, got its name from an explorer who, no doubt, got bored waiting for the next installment of a serial story and went out and discovered some things on his own.

Next you mount the Jackass, a high climb, and go on through Indian reservation country to Boston Bar, to one side of Hell Gate, where the Fraser has shown its strength, and later to Spuzzum, where there's a new bridge for you and your car, but where you should ask the old-timers how it was to swing and sway on the old suspension bridge. Spuzzum was once a Hudson's Bay Company post of importance, but flood waters have dissolved most of the history at this shelf point above the river.

Watch for places along the river where the Indians net salmon and high points on the rocks where they smoke them. "Thousands of miners and millions of treasure" passed over the Cariboo Road from Hope, the next town, says an inscription which gives a credit line to British army engineers. (In Spuzzum: Fort Hope and Commercial Hotels, Kawakawa Lake, and other auto camps.)

Agassiz is the terminal for the well-known Harrison Hot Springs and its hotel, as well as for the ferry to Chilliwack, sitting at the head of a rich agricultural valley. And thus on to New Westminster, which used to be provincial capital, was named by Queen Victoria, and is now third city of British Columbia. Vancouver is so near it steals New Westminster's civic thunder.

Route 1 goes on over to Vancouver Island (after a five-hour ferrying job to Victoria). Even the blitz-and-run types among you could spend an ordinary length vacation on this island and have plenty left over to see on yet another journey. Vancouver Island lies so far south that it actually overlaps the international boundary by about sixty miles. It is only a few hundred miles south of Alaska but is laved by warm waters which are just right to preserve the half-million British teacups owned by the 148,000 inhabitants, and provide salubrious rose-growing weather.

Victoria is residential and prim and charming, at least for awhile. It is also a sharp dividing line between two distinct attitudes on life. I know a man of eighty years who can't stand Victoria for the same reason he can't stand St. Petersburg, Florida: he says the place is cluttered up with people who have stopped thinking and producing. It is nice to have seen Victoria, just as it is nice to go back and see the polite chaos of a maiden aunt living alone in an old house full of habits and heirlooms. The streets are wide and shaded, the gardens lovely. But the streets have "queer quirks and jogs" which may delight you or anger you. The best advice seems to be to see Victoria, certainly one of the quieter provincial capitals, and then go on before you begin to agree with that class of tourist you may hear characterize this lovely city as "a well-landscaped Pompeii with conversation brought as near to date as the charge at Balaklava."

However there is no question about the courtesy of the helmeted policemen, as calm and efficient as the Bobbies of London; about the service or surroundings at the Empress Hotel, where every afternoon at teatime they are missing a great bet by not originating a "Duchess for a Day" radio program. (Also, these other good hotels with cheaper rates, which may be quite an item: The Dominion, the Strathcona, and the Douglas; and Belmont, Edgewater, Craigflower, the Farm, Home, Hillside, and Victoria auto courts.) There are scenic marine drives (since the city faces water on three sides), Mount Douglas Park, Mount Tolmie Park, and the famous Butchart Gardens.

They call Route 1 the "Island Highway." At Goldstream the Malahat Drive begins. At a nice elevation, it affords long views of the Arm, the closely farmed stretches on the Saanich ridges, then drops down to sea level at Mill Bay, through the maple groves near Cowichan, to the crossing of the Koksilah, where Robert W. Service wrote his first poem for publication. Duncan is like a hundred little English towns. Ladysmith is named for the South African battle (or siege) and is famed for its oysters. Take the right fork of the road to Nanaimo; it has a better view of the river. The town has a balcony seat over a fine bay. Ruins of an old Hudson's Bay Company fort and the resort of Newcastle Island, near by, are the sole tourist attractions. (In Nanaimo: Shangri-La, Happyland, Cascade, Nanaimo courts.)

Parksville has a good beach. A side trip through a forest of firs and cedars known as Cathedral Grove takes you thirty miles to the Albernis, at the head of Alberni Canal and in front of Mount Arrowsmith. Stamp Falls is an excellent place to see the salmon at spawning time trying to leap the cascade. Back on Route 1, Qualicum Beach is a cooling place, perhaps aided by the view it affords of snow-capped peaks across the strait. After leaving Courtenay there is a view of the Forbidden Plateau peaks. This section is another alpine wonderland of quiet lakes, snowy eminences, and even of pink snow! (A minute pink plant supplies the gimmick. Take along color film and snap pastel snowballs.) The name, a natural for tourists if there ever was one, comes from the Indians telling hard luck tales about traveling up there.

Going on, Route 1 hugs the coast to Campbell River, home of the original Tyee Club, whose roster is a *Who's Who* of famous fishermen since Walton. Side roads lead to Elk Falls, which looks like a 120-foot squirt of carbonated water, and Forbes Bay, a fishing resort (Forbes Lodge, Campbell River Guest Cottages). On to Menzies Bay, like Campbell River, a logging center, and then when the highway returns to the sea, Sayward and Kelsey Bay, fishing resorts. This is the end of the highway, which we hope will one day be extended all around the island.

Now back to Ashcroft for a peek up the Cariboo. If you are with a large party, no doubt someone will try to discover an old native coot who was alive back in 1862–65, in the hectic days of the gold rush. Chances are they'll be successful in that search, too. Unless you are a fisherman or movie-location man wanting a mining town for background shots, that may be your biggest thrill up the Cariboo Road. Near the main road are Kelly, Canim, Mahood, Horse, Horsefly, Bridge, Big Bar, Little Bar, Pavilion, Lac la Hache, Quesnel, and Stuart Lakes, all good for fly-fishing or trolling. There is a succession of little towns, some of them with Indian cowboys strolling in the streets, and endless stretches of jack pine, patches of alfalfa, roads branching off to the fishing grounds, and, finally, Prince George and Hazelton. But before that, just beyond Quesnel, you may turn off to the right and visit Barkerville, an authentic old mining town. The weathered old church, the gravel heaps which have been turned over ten times in a search for gold, the tiny gardens with the new dirt carted in from the foothills like windowsill Edens in Manhattan, the old-timers who can tell you where there's enough gold to make you rich (if they only had a stake they'd go right out and "discover" it) are the real McCoy, double-distilled.

Up at Prince George you are on the rim of the Indian

country. This is a picturesque provisioning point, a springboard for the more primitive areas above it. No longer do
the free-spending American pilots drop down from the skies,
in "the second gold rush." But someday this should be the
approach for Americans of the West Coast, to the Alaska
Highway. Before that, much road building must be accom-
plished and paid for. What remains of the highway turns
left, westerly, through beautiful canoeing country. From
Burns Lake it is possible in good weather to get fairly close
to the largest scenic park in the Dominion, Tweedsmuir. It
has 5,400 square miles, and almost all of it is said to be beautiful. However, there is no way to get about in it except by
hiking or on horseback, and once there the only accommodations are trail camps. It is definitely not a place to take
Aunt Sally, who has been used to comfort in Des Moines. A
group of hardy men who like to rough it can have a roaring
time, however, for there are competent guides with good
equipment, rare Indians to see (they almost never see white
men, according to government report), and grizzlies to shoot
along the Atnarko River.

Hazelton, the "Indian town," is about the end of the road,
although several of my friends have told me lately they had
no trouble pulling a trailer up the road that far. In this
town note the machine-made stone totem poles over the
graves, replacing the majestic wooden poles, tabooed by
the church. Possessions of the departed don't go back to
the finance company in Hazelton; they are put in a tiny
shack at the grave: Gadgets for Heaven.

THE ALASKA HIGHWAY

The Alaska Highway, four-fifths of which is in Canada
and therefore falls within the scope of this book, is the longest auto road through raw, undeveloped country that the
world has ever seen. It is 1,523 miles from Dawson Creek

to Fairbanks, and there aren't more than thirty stops ready for you in all that way. But the road itself is gravel, twenty-six feet wide, in fairly good repair almost all the time. It is a good job of engineering; the grades aren't killers.

Here is the latest available information, although this list will be growing all the time:

Mile 0, Dawson Creek, B.C.—hotels, stores, meals, gas and oil, seventy-five beds.

Mile 49, Fort St. John, B.C.—hotels, stores, meals, gas and oil, repairs, 150 beds.

Mile 101, Blueberry, B.C.—meals, gas and oil, four beds.

Mile 147, Beaton River, B.C.—store, meals, twenty beds.

Mile 201, Trutch, B.C.—meals, gas and oil.

Mile 233, Prophet River, B.C.—store, meals, twenty beds.

Mile 300, Fort Nelson, B.C.—meals, store, gas and oil, repairs, hotel, fifty beds.

Mile 392, Summit Lake, B.C.—meals, gas and oil, minor repairs, six beds.

Mile 456, Muncho Lake, B.C.—meals, gas and oil.

Mile 533, Coal River, B.C.—hotel, meals, gas and oil, ten beds.

Mile 620, Power Post, B.C.—store, meals, gas and oil, 40 beds.

Mile 634, Watson Lake, Yukon Territory—store, meals, gas and oil.

Mile 710, Rancheria, Y.T.—meals, gas and oil, ten beds.

Mile 804, Teslin, Y.T.—store, meals, gas and oil, four beds.

Mile 833, Marsh Lake, Y.T.—hotel, meals, gas and oil, thirty beds.

Mile 918, Whitehorse, Y.T.—hotel, meals, gas and oil, repairs, stores, one hundred beds.

Mile 974, Champagne, Y.T.—store, four beds.

Mile 1,016, Haines Road Junction, Y.T.—store, meals, gas and oil.

Mile 1,022, McIntosh's, Y.T.—store, meals, four beds.

Mile 1,094, Burwash Landing, Y.T.—hotel, store, meals, gas and oil, repairs, forty beds.

Mile 1,184, Dry Creek, Y.T.—hotel, meals, gas and oil, forty beds.

Mile 1,206, Snag, Y.T.—Canadian Immigration and Customs, six beds.

Mile 1,221.4—Canada-Alaska boundary.

Mile 1,226, Scottie Creek, Alaska—store, gas and oil.

Mile 1,270, Northway, Alaska—store, gas and oil.

Mile 1,318, Tok Junction, Alaska—gas and oil, meals, store, forty beds.

Mile 1,428, Big Delta, Alaska—gas and oil, meals, stop-over.

Mile 1,458, Richardson, Alaska—gas and oil, repairs, meals.

Mile 1,523, Fairbanks, Alaska—hotels, stores, meals, gas and oil.

It is anticipated that accommodations and travel facilities will have been augmented this season, particularly overnight accommodations.

All applications for permits to travel over the road must be made in person, but preliminary information can be secured by writing the Assistant Commissioner, Royal Canadian Mounted Police, Edmonton, Alberta. Certain equipment, a half dozen small items, must be carried along, and that list will be supplied. Your car must look as though it will stand the trip, and you are required to have about $200 a person in cash on you. It will take about a week each way. There's lots to see: high, remote peaks, glaciers, rushing rivers, tall timber, good fishing waters. Screen your fellow-passengers most carefully. Leave the prima donnas, the chronic complainers, the overtimorous, and the tellers of repetitious anecdotes at home. But then that's always a good general rule on just any lengthy drive—if you can get away with it.

There are hundreds of trips through the north which are being taken every summer by hardy Americans, but which are only partially possible to those not inured to hardship or ready to react quickly in the face of possible danger. There was that jaunt of my fellow-Laredoan, Eugene Burgess. He took a steamer from Seattle to Juneau ($90); a yacht, Juneau to Skagway ($17); passage ($13) from Skagway to Whitehorse on the Whitepass Railroad; the steamer Keno (five days, $42) to Dawson, where he bought a rowboat for $25 and floated down the four hundred miles to Fort Yukon. Then he sold his craft for $10 and came back to the United States. Not bad for a "Cheechako," or newcomer to the northern wastes!

"I was nine days in that rowboat," said Eugene. "Upon occasion I went as much as a hundred miles without even seeing an Indian. If I'd stoved my craft in going through some of those rapids I'd have had to walk out of there, somehow. No, it's definitely not a trip for a pantywaist, but someday, with a good partner, I'd like to do it again and really plan the thing. Columbus couldn't have had a bigger whammy in his first trip to the Indies than I got out of mine to the Arctic Circle."

· 16 ·

Farewell to the World's Greatest
Tourist Attraction

"DID YOU buy anything in Canada?" the American customs
inspector wanted to know as I went over the line from
British Columbia, headed for Seattle. "You are allowed $100
worth, duty free."

"Nothing tangible," I answered, and after quick, efficient
inspection of my personal effects he waved me on with a
smile. Going in and out of Canada is just about as easy as
it can be made if they are to keep any control on importa-
tions. I recalled how as I entered Canada a very courteous
customs official had given me a paper which identified my
typewriter and okayed my entrance into the country in a
little over sixty seconds. No passports, no fuss, everything
for the traveler's convenience—within reason. How much
more convenient than going into Mexico! (Especially for
hunters. Down there a hunter has the devil of a time getting
his guns in. Our brothers to the south have a fixed slant on
that: one gun, one revolution.)

No, I had nothing to declare for customs, but much to
"declare" about my trip: No purchases, but I had "bought"
something no one could ever take a lien on, a bit of Canada
for an invisible sachet to be worn always near the heart.
There should be an old saying, "Once you have gained summer sanctuary in Canada, all other places are put back in
their mediocre shade."

For I remember a land one-sixth larger than the United
States, containing a million square miles of forests, one-half
of the fresh water of the world, strategic raw materials which

the United States does not possess; ocean-battered headlands, deep valleys, rocky crags, clear, rushing streams and the bothans of Canadian crofters. And I remember the appeal of old Quebec, the strength of Montreal, the mills and marts, ganglia of the nation, which are Toronto, the studious deliberation, as though lawmaking should be done in college libraries, of Ottawa. Yes, and the wet freshness of Nova Scotian morning, the belly-blows of beauty of the Canadian Rockies.

These, from the colored travelog of memory: the skirl of pipes in Ingonish . . . and the town which has its private tidal wave . . . the mouldering bastion remnants of last century's strategy . . . the faith which transformed Mount Royal . . . fanning motions of wind-rippled miles of cereals extinguishing fires of hunger throughout the world . . . crystal-clear waterfalls high on shoulders of mountains where the rocks were tapped thousands of years before Moses was born . . . the mixture of mountain and island grandeur before Mount Garibaldi's eternally frosty backdrop, epitomizing the peace and the rest mankind seeks and never seems satisfyingly to find.

Out of it all, Canada emerges as the sudden first sight of a tiny, French stone village by the sea; an ice skater crisping his way through the frozen Venice of Halifax in winter; a priest taking off in an airplane mounted on pontoons to bring the "church" to parishioners; the moose which comes down to a pass in Jasper National Park, meeting all the trains and nodding at the passengers; the hippy movement of an amateur paramour (she must have been the great-granddaughter of the vivacious *jeune fille* for love of whom Lord Nelson wanted to go a.w.o.l.) on her first illicit visit to the comfortable beds of the Chateau Frontenac; hungry, rasping saws biting at next year's Sunday supplements; a tearful youth standing in the rainy arc of an outside light at Fredericton Junction, his clothing in a bulging paper suitcase tied with string, his hands nervously rubbing the down on his face so recently cupped by his Mom in farewell. . . .

This much we can all understand: Canada has something for any possible tourist; Canada is friendly; Canada is near at hand; Canada is cooler than the United States in those months when most Americans choose to take vacations; Canada is unforgettable.

Yes, you too must see Canada!

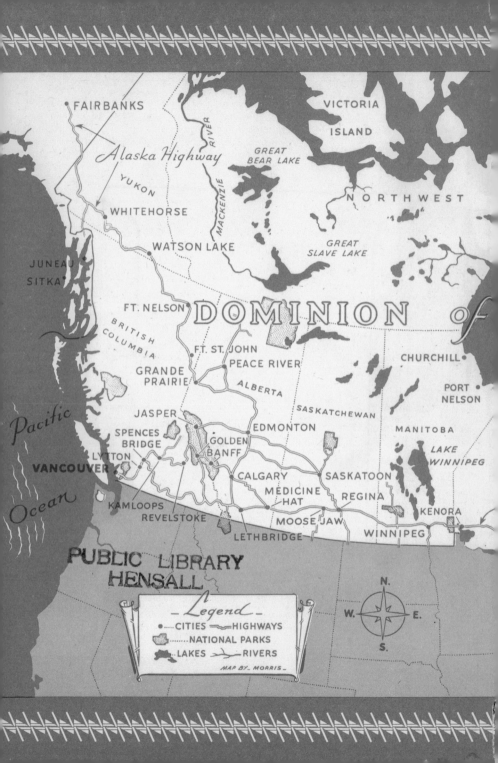